How the Spirit Became God

How the Spirit Became God

— *The Mosaic of Early Christian Pneumatology* —

Kyle R. Hughes

FOREWORD BY
Matthew W. Bates

CASCADE *Books* · Eugene, Oregon

HOW THE SPIRIT BECAME GOD
The Mosaic of Early Christian Pneumatology

Cascade Books
An Imprint of Wipf and Stock Publishers
199 W. 8th Ave., Suite 3
Eugene, OR 97401

www.wipfandstock.com

PAPERBACK ISBN: 978-1-5326-9374-8
HARDCOVER ISBN: 978-1-5326-9375-5
EBOOK ISBN: 978-1-5326-9376-2

Cataloguing-in-Publication data:

Names: Hughes, Kyle R., author. | Bates, Matthew W., foreword.

Title: How the Spirit became God : the mosaic of early Christian pneumatology / by Kyle R. Hughes ; foreword by Matthew W. Bates.

Description: Eugene, OR: Cascade Books, 2020 | Includes bibliographical references and index.

Identifiers: ISBN 978-1-5326-9374-8 (paperback) | ISBN 978-1-5326-9375-5 (hardcover) | ISBN 978-1-5326-9376-2 (ebook)

Subjects: LCSH: Holy Spirit—History of doctrines—Early church, ca. 30–600 | Holy Spirit | God (Christianity) | Theology, Doctrinal

Classification: BT119 H84 2020 (print) | BT119 (ebook)

Manufactured in the U.S.A.   04/14/20

For Karisa,

"my best beloved fellow-servant in the Lord"
Tertullian, *Ad ux.* 1.1

Come, Holy Ghost, our souls inspire,
And lighten with celestial fire;
Thou the anointing Spirit art,
Who dost thy sevenfold gifts impart.

Teach us to know the Father, Son,
And thee, of both, to be but One;
That, through the ages all along,
This may be our endless song:

Praise to thy eternal merit,
Father, Son, and Holy Spirit.

Veni, Creator Spiritus
Book of Common Prayer (1662)

Contents

List of Illustrations

Foreword

It is not often that one gets to introduce an untold theological story. It is rarer when it is a story that is theologically essential. Yet when a scholarly tale is both novel and about the central Christian mystery—the Trinity—it's akin to seeing an albino elk cross the street in downtown Los Angeles. We've moved from rare to impossible. This is what makes Kyle Hughes's *How the Spirit Became God* exciting. This book is theology proper in the deepest sense—*theo-logia*. It is a study of God's own speech as God bears witness about God's own self life. And it is largely new.

The degree to which *How the Spirit Became God* is groundbreaking, important, and likely to stimulate widespread theological conversation becomes apparent when we consider the parallel case. How did Jesus come to be regarded as God in early Christianity? Because the answer is of ultimate significance, the scholarly effort seeking to unravel the puzzle of christological origins has been prodigious.

It was once widely held that Jesus came to be regarded as God only after a lengthy developmental process. According to scholars such as Adolph von Harnack, Wilhelm Bousset, and J. D. G. Dunn, the pure Jewish monotheism of the New Testament era morphed as it collided with the polytheistic Graeco-Roman world, allowing Jesus the Son to be declared a god alongside God (the Father). Several centuries later at the Council of Nicaea, the tension inherent in this development was alleviated by declaring that there was only and ever one God, because the Son is eternally begotten of the Father yet they are the same essence.

There are few scholars today that find this developmental narrative to be a convincing account of christological origins. The problem is our earliest Christian writings—Paul's letters—already have a full-orbed divine Christology. The Son was considered God within the bounds of monotheism from the beginning. Larry Hurtado, Richard Bauckham, Gordon Fee, David Capes, Chris Tilling, Crispin Fletcher-Louis, and others have persuaded the majority that a high Christology arose very early, even if there is still disagreement over how to best model the Father-Son relationship.

Thus current scholarship by and large agrees to an early high Christology, and the frenetic pace of research on early Christology continues. But as we seek to discern the mystery of mysteries, the central dogma that makes Christianity distinctively triune but monotheistic, whence the Spirit? Christology, yes! Pneumatology, what?!? As a scholarly community, with regard to how the Spirit became God, we are like the befuddled disciples that Paul encountered in Ephesus: "We have not even heard that there is a Holy Spirit" (Acts 19:2). Given its obvious import, from a Christian origins standpoint, why has scholarship been unable to tell the story of how the Spirit came to be considered divine?

Several possible reasons for the neglect can be suggested. Perhaps the Spirit is simply an agent of God but not fully divine in the New Testament or other early Christian writings, so the story lacks foundation? Or, perhaps, there is data suggesting that the Spirit is divine (in some fashion) but our sources don't yield a plausible model for how that happened? Perhaps the second-century and third-century church has little to add about the process? Unlike with regard to Jesus, maybe the divinity of the third person of the Trinity was a very late development, since the first theological treatise fully defending the deity of the Spirit was Basil of Caesarea's *On the Holy Spirit* in the fourth century? Maybe.

Or, as Kyle Hughes shows, maybe we've been missing the pieces that would allow this story to be told, because we've failed to look at the New Testament and early church sources from the best vantage points. Maybe we need to take early Christian experiences of the Spirit with more seriousness. Maybe we need to discover the person-centered reading assumptions of the earliest Christians (e.g., *prosopological exegesis*), and see how this colored their reading of Scripture. Maybe we need to recover evidence for the Spirit as the one who bears witness to the deity of the Father and the Son—but in so doing shows that *only a divine person can bear witness to other divine persons*. Maybe we need to read our texts again with the aid of fresh models and questions as these arise from our ancient texts. In this creative yet faithful study, Kyle Hughes blazes ahead of the reader, opening up fresh pathways.

The parallel with the intense study of Christology suggests that pneumatology is vitally important to Christian origins yet still in its infancy. Kyle Hughes's seminal study will prove foundational because it opens up new spaces within which other theologians can fruitfully work. All those who love Christian theology will want to journey with him. Yet this study is not a tour of arcane facts from the distant past.

The living Spirit surely would have resisted, but Hughes could have written a dead history, merely tracing the emergence of the doctrine of the Trinity backward in time. Thankfully Hughes does not fall into this trap. He presses the question, "whence the Spirit?" not merely as a historian but also as a theologian. "The *pneuma* blows where it chooses, and you hear the sound of it, but you do not know where it comes from or where it goes" (John 3:8). On the surface, Jesus's words to Nicodemus seem to suggest that nobody can discern where the Spirit comes from. But Jesus's point is that those who are born from above (or born again) know the Spirit's heavenly origin and life-giving power—even if outsiders like Nicodemus cannot fully comprehend this. Hughes understands that his work is not merely to be a historian, but a theologian—and that the Spirit must be free to bear witness.

While the revelation of the divinity of the Spirit (as part of the Christian doctrine of God) has an origin in time, nevertheless the Spirit's divinity is not constrained by time or by our process of discovery. Ultimately the Spirit attests to an eternal relationship between Father, Son, and Spirit. The church as the temple of the Holy Spirit is caught up within this relationship too. Hughes's study encourages us to keep in step with the *pneuma*. We are exhorted to plumb the mystery, not in order to master it, but so that we can be changed when we overhear what the Spirit says about the deep things—God's very thoughts (1 Cor 2:11–13). And nothing has more transformative potential than encountering God's thoughts about God's own self, as the Spirit bears witness.

Matthew W. Bates,

Associate Professor of Theology, Quincy University;
author of *The Birth of the Trinity*

Acknowledgments

I t turns out writing a second book is no less work than writing a first, and so I am exceedingly grateful for all of those who supported me in this endeavor. This book simply would not have been possible without Michael Thomson at Wipf and Stock, whose vision called forth this particular project, and Dr. Matthew Bates, whose life and scholarship inspires my own and who has graciously written the foreword for this book. The whole staff at Cascade, and especially my editor, the Rev. Dr. Robin Parry, were wonderful partners in this project.

To my team of friends, colleagues, and students who have encouraged, supported, or inspired my work, in ways large and small, let me extend my deepest gratitude: R. J. Barthelmes, Dr. Kevin Bracher, Anne Edwards, Dr. Jeff Horner, Bryan Klein, Katie Kling, David McBride, Dave McCune, the Very Rev. Dr. Kris McDaniel, Trevor Moore, the Rev. Tripp Prince, Nathan Stevens, William Thomas, Casey Torres, and Jennifer Woods. For their love and generosity, I must again thank my parents, Bob and Stephanie Hughes, and my grandparents, Harold and Anne Hughes.

Ultimately, though, it was my wife, Karisa, who made the practical sacrifices week in and week out to give me the time I needed to finish this project. Thank you, Karisa, for believing in me and in this book. More importantly, as to the theme of this book, I am so grateful for your partnership in helping create a home in which our children, Aliya, Asher, and Judah, can come to know and love the triune God: Father, Son, and Holy Spirit. Karisa, this book is for you.

Kyle Hughes
Epiphany 2020

Timeline of Key Events and Texts

The Problem of the Holy Spirit

F or centuries, the Christian doctrine of the Trinity has perplexed artists and iconographers no less than pastors and theologians. This difficulty is arguably most profound with respect to portrayals of the Holy Spirit. For instance, one of the most familiar types of images of the Trinity, from the Middle Ages into the present day, depicts the Son sitting at the right hand of the Father, with the Spirit, portrayed as a dove, flying between them. Generally speaking, in this image the ascended Christ is easily identifiable by his position at the right hand of the Father and on account of the cross he holds. Likewise, God the Father is instantly recognizable in the form of an old man with a beard. Directly above and between them, with wings extending towards each of their faces, and with beams of light shining forth from it in all directions, a dove completes this representation of the Trinity by signifying the Holy Spirit.[1]

On the one hand, this depiction of the triune God is richly scriptural, evoking texts such as Ps 110:1, Dan 7:13, and Matt 3:16. Still, on the other hand, something feels theologically deficient about this portrayal of the Trinity. For those committed to the Christian notion that the one God exists eternally as three coequal persons, there is something striking about the Father and the Son being portrayed as men while the Spirit is portrayed as a bird. There is a sense in which this image suggests that the Father and the

---

1. One historical explanation for the development of this depiction of the Trinity is that it arose in the Latin West in the wake of the Schism of 1054, which resulted in part over the Western church's insistence that the Holy Spirit proceeded from both the Father and the Son (the so-called *filioque* doctrine). The placement of the Spirit as a dove, between the Father and the Son, therefore visually communicates this theological idea. Despite official disapproval, this form of portraying the Trinity came to be popular in the Eastern church as well. See further Cavarnos, *Byzantine Iconography*, 2:64–65; Yazykova and Luka, "Theological Principles of the Icon," 18–19.

1

Son are relatable to us in a way that the Spirit is not. While images of Christ have made the person of Christ visually present to Christians as early as the third century, and personal images of the God the Father have been popular in Western Christianity at least since the time of the Renaissance (Michelangelo's depiction of the creation of Adam perhaps being the most famous such depiction), there has been no comparable artistic tradition portraying the Spirit in similar terms.[2]

Perhaps, whether consciously or not, these observations from the world of Christian art communicate something about the way most Christians perceive the Spirit. The relational terms "Father" and "Son" suggest familiar human models that we can latch onto, but the notion of "Spirit" strikes our ears as less personal, indeed as more like the Force from the *Star Wars* films. Indeed, on the one hand, Scripture consistently portrays the Father and the Son in personal, relational terms, with the Father speaking to the Son at Christ's baptism, or with Christ teaching his disciples to pray to his Father in heaven; on the other hand, the Spirit is often portrayed in inanimate terms, capable of being "poured out" on people (Acts 2:17) or "filling" them (Acts 2:4). There is, moreover, the issue of gender: while the terms "Father" and "Son" lend themselves to the use of masculine pronouns for these two divine persons, the label "Holy Spirit" suggests an ambiguous or non-personal "it" as the most appropriate pronoun.[3] This confusion is clearly present in the pews today, as a recent survey found that only 32 percent of American evangelicals either "strongly" or "somewhat" disagreed with the statement, "The Holy Spirit is a force but is not a personal being."[4] It is not without cause,

2. Traditionally, Byzantine iconography has depicted the Holy Spirit in different forms depending on context. Thus, the Spirit is portrayed as a dove in icons depicting the baptism of Christ, as a cloud in icons of the Transfiguration, and as tongues of fire in icons of Pentecost. See further Cavarnos, *Byzantine Iconography*, 2:66–67. As will be seen in chapter 7 of this book, the Holy Spirit is given more personal form in depictions of the scene called "The Hospitality of Abraham."

3. Of course, God has neither sex nor gender, and even gendered terms such as "Father" and "Son" are to be understood as metaphorical and not reflective of God's own ontological reality. Through Christian history, the Spirit has been portrayed using masculine, feminine, and neuter gender. Pointing out the absurdity of assigning gender to God, Gregory of Nazianzus asks, "Do you take it, by the same token, that our God is a male, because of the masculine nouns 'God' and 'Father'? Is the Godhead a female, because in Greek the word is feminine? Is the word 'Spirit' neuter in Greek, because the Spirit is sterile?" (*Orat.* 31.7; trans. Williams and Wickham). In any event, arguments from grammatical gender are irrelevant for demonstrating the Spirit's personhood; see Wallace, "Greek Grammar," 97–125.

4. These findings are taken from Ligonier Ministries' State of Theology 2018 survey.

therefore, that we can speak in this chapter of the "problem" of the Holy Spirit for Christian theology; indeed, to reference the title of a recent popular book, the Holy Spirit is, for many, a "forgotten God."[5]

Of course, the tremendous growth of Pentecostal and charismatic movements, particularly in the Global South, demonstrates that the topic of the person and work of the Spirit continues to attract enormous interest in some parts of modern Christianity. Even among American evangelicals, there is no shortage of literature on what the Bible says about the Spirit or the importance of the Spirit for Christian living.[6] What appears to be missing, however, from many of these discussions of the doctrine of the Holy Spirit (that is, pneumatology) is an account of the process by which the early Christians came to recognize the Holy Spirit as the third divine person of the Trinity. The extent of this neglect is particularly noticeable in light of the enormous interest, among scholars, pastors, and even interested lay persons, in debates over the development of early Christology. Popular books written by biblical scholars such as Larry Hurtado, Bart Ehrman, and Michael Bird have introduced large numbers of readers outside of the academy to the various historical and doctrinal complexities surrounding the debates over the divinity of Christ in the early church.[7] This present book, then, intends to tell "the rest of the story" concerning the historical origins of trinitarian theology by answering the specific question of how the Spirit came to be recognized as God by the early church. Before setting out this book's specific

For more details, visit www.thestateoftheology.com. Interestingly, the survey identifies this statement as "false" because "the Holy Spirit can be grieved and lied to (Isa 63:10; Acts 5:3; Eph 4:30)" and "he can also speak (Heb 3:7–11, 10:15–17)." Thus, "[because] an impersonal force can do none of these things, so these personal characteristics indicate that the Holy Spirit must be a person." The deficient theological reasoning here only further underscores the problems with such evangelical approaches to pneumatology: this reasoning from proof-texts conveniently leaves aside passages that portray the Spirit in impersonal terms, lacks any acknowledgement that something could be assigned personal traits without it actually being a person (as in the case of, say, anthropomorphism), and does not appeal to Nicene categories or definitions for understanding divine personhood.

5. Chan, Forgotten God.

6. To give just a couple of classic examples, see Keener, Gift and Giver; Tozer, Filled with the Holy Spirit.

7. See, e.g., Hurtado, How on Earth Did Jesus Become a God?; Ehrman, How Jesus Became God; Bird, ed., How God Became Jesus.

argument, however, we must first situate it relative to other scholarly works on the subject of early Christian pneumatology.[8]

The Study of the Spirit in Recent Scholarship

Broadly speaking, this book participates in a larger scholarly conversation that seeks to unite the study of how the early church interpreted the Bible with the study of how the early church formulated its understanding of significant theological concepts such as the doctrine of God. Though this approach might seem axiomatic to some, the reality is that traditional patristics scholarship tended to marginalize the role of biblical interpretation in the development of doctrine, instead focusing on the dogmatic teachings of various church fathers.[9] Thus, traditional studies of the development of the doctrine of the Holy Spirit have been content to lay out each father's understanding of the person and work of the Spirit without reference to how these beliefs were informed by their reading of Scripture; references to Scripture are minimal in these works.[10] These studies tend to proffer a common narrative on the development of pneumatology, one that minimizes the importance of reflection on the Holy Spirit prior to the fourth century, instead identifying the most important period for the formation of pneumatology as that between the councils of Nicaea (325) and Constantinople (381). Typical is the summary of Stanley Burgess, who asserts that pneumatology was "largely undeveloped" in the pre-Nicene period as theological debates instead prioritized issues related to the person and work of the Son.[11] While Burgess acknowledges that pre-Nicene fathers such as Tertullian and Origen are important insofar as they helped identify the Spirit as part of the Trinity, his focus is on how their reflections on the Spirit came about in response to heretics who "challenged the church

---

8. Readers eager to resume the argumentative flow of the book may consider skipping to the next section, in which I take up the book's line of argument.

9. For an overview of traditional approaches to early Christian studies and the shift to emphasizing the significance of biblical interpretation for the development of theology, see Beeley and Weedman, "Study of Early Christian Biblical Interpretation," 2–8.

10. In this vein, see, e.g., Harnack, *History of Dogma*, 4:108–19; Bethune-Baker, *Early History of Christian Doctrine*, 197–231; Swete, *Holy Spirit in the Ancient Church*, 11–409. In more recent years, slightly more, although still relatively minimal, attention to Scripture can be seen in Pelikan, *Emergence of the Catholic Tradition*, 211–19; Burgess, *Ancient Christian Traditions*, 16–196.

11. Burgess, *Ancient Christian Traditions*, 12.

toward greater self-understanding."[12] While correctly identifying heresies as an important stimulant for early Christian pneumatological reflection, Burgess and this broader stream of scholarship fail to recognize how the interpretation of Scripture was central to these debates. This traditional understanding of the development of the doctrine of the Holy Spirit therefore not only marginalizes the importance of biblical exegesis but also casts pre-Nicene developments as of little importance; in particular, early figures such as the Apostolic Fathers, Justin Martyr, and even Irenaeus are disregarded as insignificant for the broader narrative. Though these works provide a helpful catalog of various early Christian understandings of the Spirit, their discrete approach to the church fathers undermines their ability to present a cohesive argument that explains how and why the Spirit came to be recognized as a distinct divine person in the early church.

Thankfully, the most recent generation of scholarship has restored analysis of early Christian biblical interpretation to the center of discussions of early Christian theological development. As Christopher Beeley and Mark Weedman have concluded, "If it was once possible to focus on the development of doctrinal formulas per se, for today's scholars a serviceable history of the trinitarian controversy must give serious attention to patterns of doctrinal exegesis."[13] The notion that biblical exegesis was central to the early debates on the nature of distinction and unity in the Godhead has yet to fully impact scholarship on the particular subject of pneumatology, although recent years have seen some initial promising moves in this direction.

The most significant recent attempt to reimagine the story of the development of early Christian pneumatology through reference to biblical interpretation was set forth in an influential series of articles published by Lewis Ayres and Michel René Barnes in 2008.[14] According to Ayres and Barnes, three distinct phases characterized early Christian reflection on the Spirit. In the first stage, Christian writers had a rather elevated view of the importance of the Spirit on account of the ideas concerning the Spirit that they adapted from contemporaneous Judaism. For instance, the Spirit was cast as Creator, Wisdom, and even Consort of God. According to this view, the writings of Irenaeus represented the high point of this Jewish-Christian

12. Burgess, *Ancient Christian Traditions*, 14.

13. Beeley and Weedman, "Study of Early Christian Biblical Interpretation," 8.

14. These articles were collectively published as Ayres and Barnes, "Pneumatology: Historical and Methodological Considerations," 163–236.

pneumatological synthesis.[15] In the second stage, however, Jewish-Christian forms of theology were increasingly rejected by a church eager to construct an identity distinct from what was then coalescing into rabbinic Judaism. Thus, views of the Spirit particularly indebted to Judaism were set aside; the Spirit was clearly subordinated to the Son and biblical texts previously interpreted as referring to the Spirit were instead applied to the person of the Son. During this stage, writers such as Tertullian and Origen developed new ideas, such as that of "order" within the Godhead, to differentiate the Son and the Spirit, resulting in a diminished view of the significance of the Holy Spirit that lasted into the middle of the fourth century.[16] Finally, in the third stage of this understanding of the development of early Christian pneumatology, pro-Nicene fathers such as Athanasius and the Cappadocians recovered and adapted some of the higher views of the Spirit found in the first stage of pneumatological development. According to this view, it is the writings of Augustine of Hippo that represent the most mature post-Nicene reflection on the person and work of the Spirit.[17] Thus, according to this view, the development of pneumatology was not a straight-line, "slow and steady" march of progress, but rather a complex story of adaptation, abandonment, and retrieval. Crucially, for Ayres and Barnes this story unfolded in light of these various early Christian exegetes' reflections on the meaning of Scripture.

This new narrative for understanding the development of early Christian pneumatology has already begun to be felt in other scholarly literature on the subject. Accounts of pneumatological debates in the fourth century are beginning to recognize the indebtedness of the arguments made at this time to exegetical moves developed in the pre-Nicene period.[18] Recent monographs emphasizing the significance of the pneumatology of Irenaeus have likewise explicitly operated within this new paradigm, generating a more robust presentation of Irenaeus' creative pneumatological vision.[19] There are, however, some deficiencies with this particular account. For instance, in highlighting the manner in which Jewish ideas concerning the Spirit were

15. For more detail, see Barnes, "Beginning and End," 170–80.

16. For more detail, see Barnes, "Beginning and End," 180–86.

17. For more detail, see Ayres, "Innovation and *Ressourcement*," 187–206; Ayres, "Augustine and Pro-Nicene Pneumatology," 207–21; Barnes, "Augustine's Last Pneumatology," 223–34.

18. See, e.g., DelCogliano et al., *Works on the Spirit*, 11–15.

19. E.g., Briggman, *Irenaeus*, 1–4, 204–5; Lashier, *Irenaeus on the Trinity*, 164–87.

accepted or rejected by these early Christian writers, this view sets aside other potentially significant trajectories of pneumatological innovation that may threaten elements of this neat three-part schema. Thus, when Barnes writes that he is "denying the thesis that 'The [Christian] doctrine of the Spirit had to be constructed from the ground up using only the materials provided by the Scriptures,'" he is surely right that the Jewish context of the first centuries mediated important ideas concerning the Spirit.[20] Still, to the extent that Barnes' approach does not focus on how the fathers he assigns to his first stage of pneumatological development crafted their views apart from Jewish approaches to the Spirit, he risks over-simplifying and even excluding some important theological innovations. Indeed, whereas Barnes' schema ascribes little importance to the pneumatological views of Justin Martyr and places Irenaeus and Tertullian in different stages, this book will demonstrate that a more expansive reading of pre-Nicene pneumatological development will necessitate some revisions to this overall schema if it is to be put forward as the best way for understanding how pneumatology evolved in the first centuries of the Christian movement. While recognizing the important insights that this revised account of early Christian pneumatology has revealed, this book focuses more on the continuities rather than discontinuities among patristic pneumatologies.

Despite this level of increased scholarly interest in the development of the doctrine of the Holy Spirit, few attempts have been made to put these various pieces together and tell the story of how the Spirit "became" God. While much excellent scholarship on early Christian pneumatology has been published since Oskar Skarsaune proclaimed in 2002 that "there is, to my knowledge, no modern full-scale monograph on the pneumatology of the early church," the need for a volume such as this one remains just as urgent.[21] Specifically, by tracing significant themes, derived from Scripture, that in concert led to the affirmation of the Spirit as a distinct divine person, we will be in position to frame a particular way of thinking about the construction of early Christian pneumatology. Along the way, we will recover the significance of exegetes such as Justin Martyr or the author of the Epistle of Barnabas that have otherwise been overlooked in

20. Barnes, "Beginning and End," 170.

21. Skarsaune, *Shadow*, 351. Most notably, see the excellent study of Morgan-Wynne, *Holy Spirit*, although this work focused on the *experience* of the Spirit in the early patristic church and was not as attentive to the intersection of Scripture and the development of early Christian pneumatology. For a survey of older scholarship on early Christian pneumatology, see Morgan-Wynne, *Holy Spirit*, 3–9.

these discussions. With this context in mind, therefore, we are now able to set out the main lines of argument that will be developed over the course of this book as we seek to identify the means by which the Holy Spirit was recognized as God in early Christianity.

Overview: Building the Mosaic of Pneumatology

Simply put, the thesis of this book is that Christians of the patristic period came to identify the Spirit as a distinct divine person alongside the Father and the Son as a result of careful reflection on Scripture, which, in this context, primarily refers to the interpretation of what Christians would call the Old Testament, in light of their lived experience of this Holy Spirit. In other words, what this book argues is that the development that took place in these early centuries concerning the doctrine of the Holy Spirit was always characterized by an essential continuity, which was the concern to ground any new pneumatological ideas in Scripture. Specifically, then, this book traces movements towards ascribing *personhood* and *divinity* to the Holy Spirit in the pre-Nicene period as a way of building the foundation for the later orthodox doctrine of the Holy Spirit. Of course, the very terms "personhood" and "divinity" threaten to plunge us into deep, problematic waters. Though these terms will be unpacked over the course of this book, it is worth acknowledging at the outset that all language about God is of necessity symbolic and figurative; in particular, when we speak of there being trinitarian "persons," this is ultimately a metaphor for a transcendent reality that human language is otherwise incapable of describing. As Matthew Bates has helpfully proposed, "when we speak of divine persons as revealed through scriptural interpretation, the *quality* of personhood envisioned is necessarily metaphorically determined."[22] Despite these caveats, the general concept of "person," as applied to the Holy Spirit, is helpful for getting at an understanding of the Spirit as having a distinct identity rather than as an impersonal energy or force.[23] In particular, we will find that early Christian exegetes' use of a reading strategy known as prosopological exegesis helped establish what we might call a normative grammar for understanding the Spirit as a distinct divine person. The conversation between scriptural exegesis and theological development at work in this crucial pneumatological

22. Bates, *Birth*, 38 (italics original).

23. See especially Oberdorfer, "The Holy Spirit—A Person?" 27–46; on the problem of trinitarian personhood more broadly, see Collins, *The Trinity*, 52–94.

development is, we will see, precisely the same dynamic taking place across the other innovations analyzed in this book.

In any event, the narrow focus of this book on specific steps towards the articulation of the Spirit as a distinct divine person means that this work will not be a comprehensive account of early Christian pneumatology.[24] Indeed, vast amounts of early Christian references to the Spirit, even entire biblical books and church fathers, will be set aside in favor of a more nuanced exploration of those key movements by which the Spirit became God. While some of this story will likely be known to those familiar with the field of early Christian studies, I suspect that other parts will be new even to readers within the academy. In particular, to the extent that this book places a significant emphasis on the utilization of the aforementioned ancient reading strategy of prosopological exegesis as a major driver of the development of early Christian pneumatology, this book aims to break new ground and further advance the conversation around pre-Nicene contributions to this important yet often neglected aspect of trinitarian theology. In sum, this book aims to provide a cohesive narrative in which careful reflection on the biblical text presses early Christian exegetes, from the New Testament through the fourth century, into articulating a view of the Spirit that increasingly recognizes the Spirit's personhood and full divinity. To that end, the argument of this book will unfold over the course of the following chapters:

In chapter 2, I introduce the theme of the Spirit's provision of divine testimony, with special attention to the New Testament. Within the New Testament, the Johannine portrayal of the Spirit as the Paraclete most clearly and consistently endows the Spirit with a measure of personhood. Of particular interest for later pneumatological developments is how the Paraclete is identified as the source of divine testimony; accordingly, the exegesis of passages such as John 15:26–27 and 1 John 5:6–9 will be a central concern of this chapter. This Johannine linking of the Spirit with divine testimony would go on to pave the way for later writers to conceive of the Spirit's prosopological speech and revelation of the divine economy.

In chapter 3, we explore the theme of the Spirit and Christian identity, examining the Spirit's "capture" by Christians in their struggle for a distinctive identity over and against Judaism. This chapter devotes special attention to the Epistle of Barnabas and Justin Martyr in order to introduce and

---

24. Many such excellent introductions to the study of pneumatology as a whole include Cole, *He Who Gives Life*; Castelo, *Pneumatology*; Kärkkäinen, *Pneumatology*; Kärkkäinen, *Holy Spirit*; Holmes, *Holy Spirit*.

demonstrate the role that the conflict with Judaism played in developing a distinctively Christian understanding of the Spirit. Indeed, because the Old Testament and the Holy Spirit were identified as the exclusive possessions of the Christians, Christians were thereby positioned to find evidence of the Spirit speaking about Christ and the Father in the Old Testament, as in the case of prosopological exegesis.

In chapter 4, the focus shifts to the theme of the Spirit's emergence as a distinct divine person. Through an examination of the ancient reading strategy of prosopological exegesis and its application in the writings of Justin Martyr, Irenaeus, and Tertullian, we will trace the emergence of the Spirit as a distinct person capable of conversing with the Father and the Son. For their parts, Justin and Irenaeus focus their identification of the Spirit's prosopological speech on instances in which the Spirit provides testimony to the divinity and lordship of the Father and the Son. Tertullian, however, severs the link between the Spirit's prosopological speech and divine testimony, setting up the discussion in the following chapter on the Spirit's role in revealing the divine economy.

In chapter 5, we take up the theme of the Spirit's revelation of the divine economy, with special attention given to key passages in the writings of Irenaeus, Tertullian, and Origen. As such, we are introduced to the early Christian conception of the divine economy as a way of thinking about God's plan of salvation for the human race and the Spirit's role in communicating this economy to human beings. While especially in Tertullian this theme stands independent of the Spirit's prosopological speech, both Irenaeus and Tertullian connect the Spirit's revelation of the economy with that early notion of the Spirit as one who provides divine testimony. For his part, Origen extends this idea to describe the Spirit as having been eternally present alongside the Father and the Son, contributing to later defenses of the Spirit's full divinity even as he continues to promote a subordinationism that would be utilized by those who opposed such an understanding of the Spirit.

In chapter 6, our historical investigation concludes with an examination of the fourth-century debates over the Spirit's full divinity. Through a close reading of key texts by Athanasius, Didymus the Blind, and Basil of Caesarea, we explore the pro-Nicene articulation of the full divinity of the Holy Spirit in the context of the Pneumatomachian controversy. While examining how these pro-Nicene writers developed new arguments for the Spirit's full divinity appropriate for their own context, we will also explore the extent to which we may observe continuity in pneumatological development insofar as these writers built on the themes found in the previous chapters to solidify the orthodox doctrine of the Holy Spirit as a distinct divine person.

Finally, in chapter 7, I aim to set out some scholarly and pastoral implications of the view of the Spirit articulated in this book. Accordingly, a major focus is on drawing from the church fathers encountered in this book to recover a fully trinitarian view of the Christian life and worship, one in which the Spirit invites us to participate in the life of the triune God by instructing us in the mysteries of the divine economy as we grow in holiness and in our capacity to contemplate God. Thus, this book concludes with an attempt to show why attention to the historical process by which the Spirit became God can inform our view of the Spirit and our interaction with the Spirit today. It is only fitting, after all, that a book that begins by discussing the "problem" of the Holy Spirit concludes with an invitation to engage with this Spirit in a way that is deeply grounded in the riches of the Christian tradition.

As the reader will observe, this book proceeds thematically rather than through a study of each individual text or church father. Each approach has its value, but in seeking to understand how the Spirit became God, we are best served by analyzing the various key elements that furthered the development of early Christian pneumatology, keeping the focus on the book's overall argument and not simply providing disconnected summaries of each individual writer's view of the Spirit. As for how these different themes cohere and relate to one another, I would like to suggest the image of a mosaic as a helpful, albeit limited and imperfect, metaphor. I propose that the development of early Christian pneumatology can be understood by thinking of each pneumatological theme as an individual tile making up the full mosaic, centuries in the making, of the pro-Nicene conception of the personhood and divinity of the Holy Spirit. In particular, we may note that each tile of a mosaic, when set, dictates the selection and placement of future tiles. In the same way, as new ways of thinking about the Spirit were adopted, this both limited potential future ideas about the Spirit and established the pattern for subsequent themes to continue. While each individual tile-layer may not have understood what the end product of the mosaic would be, they did recognize the need to lay their tiles in continuity with what had been set before their time, to further elaborate the basic image that was gradually coming into focus. A fundamental element of this continuity, I will argue in this book, is that each tile was ultimately cut from the same source: the pages of Scripture, primarily meaning what we call the Old Testament. Just as an artist creating a mosaic would have used different colored tiles of the same material, so the various pneumatological ideas incorporated into the mosaic of the Holy Spirit were of a similar substance, preserving a basic unity even amidst the diversity of different colors or themes. A second element of continuity that we will track throughout this book is that each tile is placed in the mosaic via a shared adhesive: the actual lived experience of the Holy Spirit. Though the nature of this experience would take different forms over the centuries, it was nevertheless the case that no tile was added to the mosaic without a firm belief in the Spirit as living and active in the lives of believers. At the end of each chapter, then, we will want to step back and observe how this mosaic is taking shape.

Before proceeding to the core of the book, two final orienting comments are needed. First, concerning the audience of this book, I have aimed, as far as possible, to make this narrative accessible to a broad audience. Beyond students in graduate or seminary courses on the history of doctrine or early Christian theology, I hope that scholars, pastors, and even interested lay persons may find this book useful and thought-provoking. Many of the ideas explored in this book were first examined in my monograph *The Trinitarian Testimony of the Spirit: Prosopological Exegesis and the Development of Pre-Nicene Pneumatology* (Brill, 2018), which was a revision of my doctoral dissertation. Readers who desire a more scholarly analysis of some of the items in this book, especially the subject of prosopological exegesis from the person of the Holy Spirit, should consult this earlier volume. This present book, however, not only aims to be accessible to a broader audience but also broadens the focus from the particular subject of prosopological exegesis to the greater story of how the Spirit became God. Thus, while those familiar with my *Trinitarian Testimony* will hear echoes of arguments made in that volume, the vastly different scope and program of this book allows it to stand entirely on its own.

Second, a few words must be said about the dual nature of the task at hand. On the one hand, this book is primarily a historical investigation that seeks to understand, on their own terms, the process by which early Christian exegetes looked to Scripture for constructing their view of the person and work of the Spirit. As a historian, my interest is not so much in evaluating whether or not the fathers' reading of the Scripture is "right" or "wrong" in some absolute sense; rather, my task is to explain "how" and "why" the Spirit came to be recognized as a distinct divine person. This is truly the story, therefore, of how the Spirit became God. On the other hand, I write this book from the standpoint of a professing Christian. As an ordained deacon within the Anglican Church of North America, I believe, with the creeds of Nicaea and Constantinople, that there is one God who eternally subsists as three distinct persons—Father, Son, and Holy Spirit. From this perspective, the Holy Spirit has always been God, and thus to speak of "how the Spirit became God" may appear inappropriate in light of the Spirit's eternal existence as part of the triune God. As such, the reader should understand the title of this book not as an ontological statement concerning the origins of the Spirit's divinity, but rather as a shorthand for "how the Spirit came to be recognized as God by human beings who had not previously known the Spirit to be a distinct divine person in the sense of Nicene orthodoxy" (which is, admittedly, a much less catchy title for a book).[25] I recognize that some readers may approach this topic from more of a purely historical lens, while others will join me in viewing this topic from a confessional perspective. In any event, I trust that readers from all backgrounds will find this book to be an illuminating study that casts light on a subject that is often in the shadow of the more popular subject of Christology. We begin our journey with a look at the first tiles placed in the mosaic of early Christian pneumatology.

25. The title's echo of Bart Ehrman's book *How Jesus Became God* is deliberate, with this work aiming to extend interest in the development of Christology to the study of pneumatology, which as noted above has not until now seen a similar attempt made to trace the origins of Christian belief in the distinct divine personhood of the Holy Spirit.

CHAPTER 2

The Spirit and Divine Testimony

I n the beginning was the Spirit. That is to say, historians seeking to account for the initial emergence of Christianity are on solid ground when
they observe that it was not so much a doctrine or a creed that animated
the birth of the Christian church. Rather, as James Dunn has demonstrated, "Christianity understood itself in the first instance as a religion of
the Spirit."[1] While our earliest accounts of the birth of the messianic and
charismatic sect of Second Temple Judaism that would come to be known
as Christianity date to several decades after the events they recount would
have taken place, we can confidently say that the earliest Christians identified themselves as people who believed that they had experienced the
risen and exalted Christ through the Holy Spirit.[2] From Luke's accounts of
Pentecost (Acts 2:1–27) and the gentile mission (Acts 10:44–48) to what
we know of Paul's churches (1 Cor 12:13; Eph 4:3–4; Phil 2:1) and the
Johannine community (John 16:7–14; 1 John 4:13), we find that the shared
experience of the Spirit was at the center of these early Christian communities' identities. According to the New Testament witness, the Spirit was
responsible for ecstatic experiences (Acts 2:2–4) and charismatic gifts such
as inspired speech, healing, miracles, prophecy, and speaking in tongues
(1 Cor 12:8–10).[3] In his excellent study of the experience of the Holy Spirit
in the early church, John Morgan-Wynne identifies three central components

1. Dunn, *Beginning from Jerusalem*, 171. Dunn has done more than perhaps any
other scholar to highlight the importance of the Spirit for Jesus and early Christianity, and I would encourage readers interested in this topic to explore his works in more
detail, especially his classic *Jesus and the Spirit*.

2. Dunn, *Beginning from Jerusalem*, 164–70; cf. Kärkkäinen, *Pneumatology*, 25: "the
pouring out of the Spirit . . . propelled the birth of the Christian community."

3. Dunn, *Jesus and the Spirit*, 95–342; cf. Morgan-Wynne, *Holy Spirit*, 9–11.

at the heart of what it meant to experience the Spirit: an ecstatic sense of God's presence, illumination regarding God's purposes and divine truth, and ethical empowering for the formation of Christian character.[4]

This experience of the Spirit likely contributed to theological reflection on how Jesus' recent life, death, resurrection, and ascension should be interpreted. As N. T. Wright observes, early Christian language about the Spirit was less "a mere logical, or even a theological, deduction from fixed premises and ancient texts," and more "the language of *experience*," such that their experience of the Spirit led the first Christians to believe that prophecy was being fulfilled and the eschatological age had begun.[5] This early process of theological interpretation is seen in the New Testament writings themselves, of course, such as in the Lukan account of Peter's Pentecost sermon (Acts 2:14–41), which cites Pentecost as the fulfillment of the prophecy of Joel 2:28–32. Thus, the experience of the Spirit appears to have led to the process of reflecting on the identity and significance of that Spirit, a process by which this coalescing messianic sect of Second Temple Judaism would have logically turned to the Jewish Scriptures and other Jewish writings for understanding.

That this would be the case is supported by a parallel phenomenon regarding the development of Christology. In light of their experience of Jesus' resurrection and ascension, the disciples struggled to understand how Jesus was in some sense divine and yet distinct from the God he called Father, all the while still seeking to preserve the biblical monotheism that, as Jews, they had inherited. As Larry Hurtado has compellingly argued, "an adequate historical understanding of early Christianity requires us to give significant attention to the religious experiences that obviously formed such a major part of the early Christian ethos."[6] For Hurtado, the conviction of Jesus' followers that they had had revelatory experiences of the risen Christ is a necessary factor in explaining how traditional Jewish monotheism could be altered to allow for Christ to be included with God as a recipient of devotion and worship.[7] In light of these experiences (cf.

4. Morgan-Wynne, *Holy Spirit*, 17–18.

5. Wright, *New Testament and the People of God*, 446 (italics original); see also Dunn, *Beginning from Jerusalem*, 165–66.

6. Hurtado, *Lord Jesus Christ*, 66; see also Johnson, *Religious Experience in Earliest Christianity*; Juel, *Messianic Exegesis*.

7. Hurtado, *Lord Jesus Christ*, 70–74. Hurtado (*Lord Jesus Christ*, 72) underscores that "whether one chooses to consider these particular experiences as hallucinatory, projections of mental processes of the recipients, or the acts of God, there is every reason to

1 Cor 15:5–8), Hurtado argues, "believers turned to the scriptures of the Jewish tradition to find resources for understanding Jesus and for expressing and defending their claims about his significance."[8] If, therefore, we have good reason to believe that Christology developed in light of the first Christians' experience of the risen Christ and their subsequent reflection on Scripture, we should not be surprised to find the development of pneumatology following a similar pattern. That this would be the case is only further illustrated by the close link between the experience of the Spirit and the experience of the risen Christ; as Dunn concludes with respect to Paul's witness, "The risen Jesus may not be experienced independently of the Spirit, and any religious experience which is not in character and effect an experience of Jesus Paul would not regard as a manifestation of the life-giving Spirit."[9] In other words, the experience of the Spirit was seen as in some sense an experience of Christ, and our efforts to separate these two forms of experience do not adequately reflect how the early Christians would have perceived them. Thus the project of early Christian reflection on their experience of the Spirit could not take place apart from their reflection on their experience of the risen Christ. This, by the way, suggests a potential further reason for the relatively slow development of pneumatological reflection in the early church insofar as the early Christians' worship of Christ alongside of God posed the most immediate theological problem in light of their commitment to monotheism.

To return to the Spirit more specifically, it is not surprising then that the various early Christian communities created different ways of speaking about and understanding this Holy Spirit. Indeed, a close examination of the New Testament reveals a variety of approaches to the Holy Spirit. On account of this diversity, most treatments of New Testament pneumatology present a book-by-book, author-by-author, or even theme-by-theme approach to the subject.[10] Given the existence of these more encyclopedic accounts and per the overall thesis of this book, this chapter will focus on the New Testament portrayals of the Spirit that most lend themselves to pointing in the direction of understanding the Spirit as a distinct divine

---

see them as the ignition points for the christological convictions linked to them."

8. Hurtado, *Lord Jesus Christ*, 565. On these resurrection appearances, see further Dunn, *Jesus and the Spirit*, 95–134, 144–46.

9. Dunn, *Jesus and the Spirit*, 323.

10. See, e.g., Cole, *He Who Gives Life*, 149–277; Thiselton, *Holy Spirit*, 33–160; Castelo, *Pneumatology*, 36–43.

person. First, though, we need to set out the broader New Testament perspective on this issue of the Spirit's personhood.

The question of the extent to which the New Testament portrays the Holy Spirit as a person is complicated by the aforementioned diversity of pneumatological approaches found in the New Testament itself. This, of course, reflects the wide variety of ideas concerning the Spirit that were drawn from contemporary Jewish pneumatological traditions. The writings of Paul demonstrate this point well. On the one hand, Paul often applies to the Spirit verbs that would seem to require a personal agent as the subject. For instance, in one passage Paul declares that the Spirit "helps us in our weakness," because the Spirit "intercedes for the saints"; in fact, God "knows what is the mind of the Spirit" (Rom 8:26–27). As Gordon Fee observes, "Whatever else, this is the language of personhood, presuppositionally so, and not that of an impersonal influence or power."[11] On the other hand, Paul also uses impersonal language to describe the Spirit, especially in regards to the Spirit's reception by believers. Thus, God "gives his Holy Spirit" (1 Thess 4:8), placing the Spirit "in our hearts" (2 Cor 1:22) as the means by which "God's love has been poured into" them (Rom 5:5). To resolve this tension, one scholar has suggested that Paul may not view the Spirit as a full person, but nevertheless views the Spirit as having "personal traits."[12] My own sense is that Paul, over the course of his writings, moves in the direction of a more personal understanding of the Spirit even as he at times maintains a more impersonal view. In the same way that we cannot expect Paul to have understood or articulated in the language of later patristic theology a view of Christ as the second person of the ontological Trinity, neither would it make sense for Paul to have set forth a pro-Nicene view of the Spirit, though of course the argument could be made that the *seeds* for these later developments of doctrine were planted in Paul's own writings.

Indeed, part of the issue for Paul, as well as for other New Testament and early Christian writers, seems to have been a difficulty in distinguishing between the Son and the Spirit. This phenomenon is described in the literature as "Spirit Christology," in which the function and even the identity of the Son and the Spirit overlap such that we can better speak of early Christian "binitarianism" than trinitarianism.[13] For Paul, as elsewhere

11. Fee, *God's Empowering Presence*, 831.

12. Rabens, *Holy Spirit and Ethics*, 144–45.

13. While some use the term Spirit Christology only "to designate the use of 'pneuma' language for Christ" (Bucur, *Angelomorphic Pneumatology*, xxvii), I am adopting the

in the New Testament, Christ and the Spirit are at times so deeply linked that they become indistinguishable. For instance, Paul refers to the "Spirit of Christ" (Rom 8:9; Phil 1:19) and the "Spirit of [God's] Son" (Gal 4:6); Christ is even described in one place as "a life-giving spirit" (1 Cor 15:45).[14] This close association of the Spirit and Christ complicated an older, simpler view in which the Spirit was a manifestation of God's power.[15] This Spirit Christology would prove to be a major impediment in the recognition of the Spirit as a distinct divine person.[16]

If it is the case, therefore, that New Testament references to the personhood of the Spirit are inconsistent and underdeveloped, it is nevertheless true that the most clearly personal portrayal of the Spirit as a person is found in the Johannine description of the Holy Spirit as the Paraclete.[17] As we consider how the Johannine presentation of the Spirit as the Paraclete casts the Spirit in strongly personal terms, we will also uncover how the identity and nature of this Paraclete is both deeply rooted in scriptural (that is, Old Testament) imagery and points forward towards later understandings of the Spirit by emphasizing the Spirit's provision of divine testimony.

The Johannine Writings

Any discussion of the experience of the Holy Spirit in early Christianity must consider the witness of the Johannine community, which we are able to partially reconstruct through the Gospel and Epistles of John.[18] Even a cursory reading of the Johannine literature reveals that the Spirit was at the center of the theology and experience of this group of early Christ-followers.[19]

---

more expansive sense of Spirit Christology as a term for "denoting the integral connection between Jesus and Spirit" (Kärkkäinen, *Pneumatology*, 18 n. 13).

14. Kärkkäinen, *Pneumatology*, 19. For an alternate view that critiques the scholarly notion of Spirit Christology, see Fee, *God's Empowering Presence*, 831–45.

15. Burge, *Anointed Community*, 49.

16. Kärkkäinen, *Pneumatology*, 35: "As long as the Spirit was not differentiated from the Son as a separate 'person,' it was difficult to say whether the Spirit was the power or influence of the Father (filling or empowering the Son) or something less than a person."

17. As argued by Kärkkäinen (*Pneumatology*, 15), the Paraclete is "the first and only personal image" of the Holy Spirit in the Bible, as opposed to its portrayal as wind, fire, water, a cloud, or a dove; while it "points to personality" it still "does not demand that the Holy Spirit be a separate *hypostasis*."

18. This section builds upon my discussion in Hughes, *Trinitarian Testimony*, 81–87.

19. See Morgan-Wynne, *Holy Spirit*, 22–44.

According to these writings, the Spirit anointed Jesus at his baptism, remained on him over the course of his ministry, and was released at the time
of Jesus' death and glorification to then likewise anoint and remain upon
Jesus' followers, with the experience of the Spirit providing direct access to
the presence of the risen Christ.[20] This experience of the Spirit took place
first and foremost through the sacraments of baptism and Eucharist, as well
as through the Spirit's work of revelation that empowered the community's
mission and witness in the world.[21] A central part of this broader pneumatology is John's description of the work of the Paraclete, interwoven into his
account of Jesus' final words to his followers.

Near the end of John's Gospel, the Evangelist presents Jesus speaking
a "farewell discourse" to his followers. In this passage (John 13:31—16:33),
Jesus unpacks the nature of his ministry and prepares his disciples for his
impending departure from this world. A central element of this extended
monologue is Jesus' introduction of a figure known as the Paraclete, referenced five times across this passage. According to Jesus, the Father will
send, at his request, a Paraclete, known as the "Spirit of truth," who will
abide with his disciples (John 14:16–17). This Paraclete is none other than
the Holy Spirit, who will be sent by the Father to teach the disciples in
Jesus' absence (John 14:26).[22] As will be explored in more detail below, this
Paraclete will testify on Jesus' behalf, serving as a model for the testimony
that will be provided by his followers (John 15:26–27). It is actually better
for his disciples, Jesus claims, that he depart, because he will then be able
to send them this Paraclete, who will convict the world about sin, righteousness, and judgment (John 16:7–11). Finally, this Paraclete will lead
Jesus' disciples into all truth, taking what belongs to the Son and declaring
it to Jesus' disciples (John 16:13–15). In sum, Raymond Brown concludes,
"the basic functions of the Paraclete are twofold: he comes to the disciples

---

20. Burge, *Anointed Community*, 223; Burge (*Anointed Community*, 150) points towards 1 John 4:13 as a succinct statement of this theme. Cf. Morgan-Wynne, *Holy Spirit*,
26, on John 7:39: "experience of the risen, exalted Jesus and his life-giving power was the
experience of the Holy Spirit."

21. Burge, *Anointed Community*, 224.

22. Elsewhere in the Farewell Discourse, the Paraclete is sent by Christ rather than
the Father (as at John 15:26 and 16:7), which is best understood as reflecting the "tight
cohesion of the Father and the Son" (Carson, *John*, 499). Keener (*John*, 2:1022) writes
that "early Christians probably regarded the alternatives as complementary rather than
contradictory," pointing to Gal 4:6. On the extension of this problem to the issue of the
filioque, see Carson, *John*, 528–29.

and dwells within them, guiding and teaching them about Jesus; but he is hostile to the world and puts the world on trial."[23]

The best way to make sense of this teaching about the Paraclete is to place it within the broader lens of the Fourth Gospel's so-called "trial motif." In his Gospel, John not only presents Jesus as on trial before his contemporaries but also portrays the world as on trial before God, with Jesus cast as the witness providing the most important testimony.[24] As Burge notes, "Initially this lawsuit is presented on a historical level as Jesus debates with the Jews, but in addition, readers are forced to adjudge the case for themselves and assess the validity of the Evangelist's verdict (20:31)."[25] This motif is extended to the Paraclete in the Farewell Discourse, as is most clearly stated by Jesus in John 15:26–27: "When the Advocate [Paraclete] comes, whom I will send to you from the Father, the Spirit of truth who comes from the Father, he will testify on my behalf. You also are to testify because you have been with me from the beginning." Here, the Paraclete works alongside the disciples to testify about Jesus to the world. To put it another way, Jesus' trial before the world will continue even after his departure and even as the church experiences persecution from the world, necessitating the presence of the Paraclete.

This understanding of the legal (or "juridical") work of the Paraclete helps us supply an appropriate English gloss for this Greek title. While it has been popular to render Paraclete as "Comforter," D. A. Carson points out that in modern English this "sounds like a quilt or like a do-gooder at a wake," failing to capture the legal context at work.[26] Thus, a better translation of the primary meaning of this term is almost certainly "Advocate," in the sense of a legal assistant.[27] Specifically, the forensic function of the Spirit is to serve both as a witness defending Jesus and as his spokesman over the course of his trial by the world.[28] Still, some scholars recommend simply leaving "Paraclete" untranslated, recognizing that even this legal image does not capture the fullness of the Johannine portrayal, with the Paraclete also

23. Brown, *John XIII–XXI*, 1136; cf. Keener, *John*, 2:1021–25.

24. See Burge, *Anointed Community*, 204–8; for more thorough studies on the Johannine trial motif, see Harvey, *Jesus on Trial*; Bekken, *Lawsuit Motif*; Lincoln, *Truth on Trial*.

25. Burge, *Anointed Community*, 205.

26. Carson, *John*, 499.

27. See further Lincoln, *John*, 393–94.

28. Brown, *John XIII–XXI*, 1136; cf. Burge, *Anointed Community*, 208–11.

tasked with consoling and teaching the disciples in Jesus' absence.[29] Indeed, one new approach to understanding the role of the Paraclete, sensitive to the significance of ancient patron-client relationships, has emphasized the manner in which the Paraclete makes Jesus and his patronage more widely available following his departure.[30] Other scholars have additionally brought attention to how the Paraclete functions as an anamnesis, helping believers recall, interpret, and apply Jesus' teachings, which appears to even be inclusive of future revelation (John 14:26, 16:13).[31]

While recognizing the complexity of the Johannine portrayal of the functions of this Paraclete, it is the Paraclete's role as Advocate that is most significant for the overall thesis of this book and will therefore receive our attention below. We will examine, in turn, how this depiction of the Paraclete introduces the motif of divine testimony, establishes an element of distinct personhood, and relates back to ideas found in the Old Testament.

The Testimony of the Paraclete

The Johannine presentation of the Paraclete sets up an enormously important idea that will be of great significance for later Christian writers' theology of the Holy Spirit. One of the central aspects of the Paraclete's work, according to the Farewell Discourse, is that the Paraclete will "testify" on Jesus' behalf after his departure. Interestingly, whereas the disciples will testify *about* Jesus (John 15:27), the Paraclete testifies *for* Jesus (John 15:26). The content of this testimony appears to center on proper understanding of Jesus' person and work; the "Spirit of truth" presumably leads believers to knowledge of Jesus and his teaching (John 16:13).[32] Moreover, because the Paraclete is the "Spirit of truth," Jesus' disciples can rest assured that the Paraclete's testimony is true. The reason for this is the Spirit's intimate union with Jesus, who is himself elsewhere in John's Gospel described as "the truth" (John 14:6).

---

29. Brown, *John XIII–XXI*, 1136.

30. See further Brown, *Spirit in the Writings of John*, 196. Thus, we should note, with Burge (*Anointed Community*, 9), that "the variety of traits given to the Paraclete defy any attempt to give him a comprehensive title."

31. For various attempts at making sense of the possibility of further revelation from the Paraclete, see the discussions in Burge, *Anointed Community*, 211–17; Dunn, *Jesus and the Spirit*, 351–53; cf. Morgan-Wynne, *Holy Spirit*, 30–33.

32. See further Brown, *Spirit in the Writings of John*, 200; Breck, *Spirit of Truth*, 164.

Turning to another passage in the Johannine corpus can help fill in more of the details concerning the Spirit's testimony. In 1 John 5, John is describing the power of faith and calling his audience to boldness and holiness, challenging false views about the nature of Jesus' incarnation.[33] For John, a person who believes that Jesus is the Son of God "conquers the world" (1 John 5:4–5). The reason believers know this to be the case, despite the outward circumstances of division or persecution that may seem to indicate otherwise, is the testimony of God (1 John 5:6–12). Specifically, on the nature of this testimony, John describes three independent witnesses to Jesus' identity as the Son of God that are in agreement: the water, the blood, and the Spirit (1 John 5:6–8). By the "water" and the "blood," John likely has in mind Jesus' baptism and death, both of which revealed him to be the Christ.[34] The third witness, the Spirit, is here described as "truth," echoing John 15:26. As in John's Gospel, the Spirit's witness is to the person and work of Jesus, revealing Jesus as having come in the flesh from God (1 John 4:2). Indeed, the emphasis appears to be, as in the Gospel of John, on how the Spirit is released only following Jesus' death.[35]

This passage in the epistle goes beyond that in the Gospel in two significant ways. First, 1 John 5:6 portrays the testifying role of the Spirit as a present reality, whereas John 15:26–27 envisioned this testifying as a future action. This makes sense insofar as the Johannine community believed that the Holy Spirit had been poured out upon them in line with Jesus' promise (1 John 4:13). Second, John here identifies the testimony of God as "greater" than that of human beings (1 John 5:9). When John refers to the testimony of God, he probably does not have in mind the three witnesses described in 1 John 5:6–8; rather, the reference appears to be the witness of the Father (John 5:37).[36] John's emphasis on the significance of the testimony of

33. Burge, *Anointed Community*, 95.

34. See further Painter, *1, 2, and 3 John*, 303–6; for a contrasting view, see Lieu, *I, II, and III John*, 205–15. On the myriad textual problems in this passage, and especially the later insertion of the so-called "Johannine Comma," see Metzger, *Textual Commentary*, 647–49. In commenting on the addition of the Comma, Painter (*1, 2, and 3 John*, 308) identifies this as "an excellent example of the way the wording of the text of NT writings provoked theological development in the early centuries." This is, of course, very much in line with the overall thesis of this book.

35. Burge, *Anointed Community*, 96. On this passage, see also Morgan-Wynne, *Holy Spirit*, 41–42.

36. This may in turn be a reference to the words spoken from heaven at Jesus' baptism and transfiguration (cf. Mark 1:11, 9:7). See further Painter, *1, 2, and 3 John*, 309–10; Lieu, *I, II, and III John*, 216–18; *contra* Kruse, *Letters of John*, 181, who identifies the testimony of God as the testimony of the eyewitness through whom God is speaking.

God, for an ancient audience, would have invoked what scholars of classical rhetoric refer to as the motif of divine testimony.

In Greco-Roman rhetoric, a forensic argument was assembled on the basis of various forms of proofs.[37] One of the most important of these proofs was known as "divine testimony," which generally had the function of portraying a character as either pious or impious.[38] For an ancient rhetorician, divine testimony was a particularly persuasive proof because of the weight of divine authority, and appeals to divine testimony can be found throughout ancient speeches, treatises, and even narratives. This aspect of classical rhetoric carried into the writing of the New Testament and other early Christian literature. For example, in the Gospel of Luke, the scene at Jesus' baptism (Luke 3:21–22), featuring the voice from heaven and the descent of the Spirit in the form of a dove, would have been readily recognized by an ancient audience as an appeal to divine testimony in support of the notion of Jesus as a pious figure.[39] Divine testimony could take the form of either words or deeds, and this particular example thus draws on both to clearly mark Jesus as a figure who has received divine approval, encouraging the reader of Luke's Gospel to recognize and affirm Jesus as the protagonist of the story, enjoying God's favor and innocent of the charges made against him.

To return to 1 John 5:9, we can now recognize this as a clear instance of an appeal to the proof of divine testimony. Even though in this particular instance the divine testimony being referenced is that of the Father to the Son, the fact that this claim immediately follows the appeal to the testimony of the Spirit to the Son likely further stimulated the development of the early Christian understanding of the Spirit's testifying role. After all, even assuming that John would not have understood the Spirit to be fully God in the Nicene sense,[40] the Spirit would nevertheless fall on the God-side of the division between God and human beings established in this passage. Thus, one

37. The technical word here is *topos*, which McConnell (*Divine Testimony*, 24) defines as "a source of proofs, used in composing a speech for the purposes of defending or prosecuting someone accused of some crime."

38. McConnell, *Divine Testimony*, 72–73: "Specifically, orators often applied this form of testimony in order to praise one's client, or, conversely, to denigrate an opponent. Likewise, the testimony of the gods was used to demonstrate the gods' support or lack thereof for a potential course of action."

39. McConnell, *Divine Testimony*, 232–35.

40. Lieu (*I, II, and III John*, 215) notes that the Spirit is listed alongside the water and the blood in 1 John 5:6–8 but not alongside the Father and the Son in 1 John 5:9–12.

could reasonably infer that the testimony of the Spirit is greater than that of any human being, particularly insofar as the Spirit's testimony is guaranteed to be true (1 John 5:6). This lines up neatly with how divine testimony functions more generally. Therefore, when Jesus claims that the Spirit will testify on his behalf (John 15:26), it is only natural that he appeals to the Spirit's union with the Father and hence divine nature (however that is conceived of at this point in time) and the truthfulness of the Spirit's testimony. By invoking the Spirit as the source of divine testimony to the person and work of Jesus, John has set the foundation for later, critical pneumatological innovations, as will be explored in subsequent chapters of this book.

What is lacking from John's account of the Spirit's provision of divine testimony is any explanation of *how* the Spirit thus testifies.[41] Particularly noteworthy is the absence of any explicit appeal to the Spirit's relationship to Scripture. As James McConnell has demonstrated, the ancient notion of divine testimony through utterances included the category of oracles, and Luke, in his Gospel and in Acts, seems to use quotations from and allusions to the Old Testament in the same way that Greco-Roman narratives employed oracles. In both cases, an ancient audience would recognize these as divine speech, set off by introductory statements, which characterized a person as either pious or impious.[42] Accordingly, McConnell claims, this kind of testimony enables the audience "to experience the divine perspective of the character in question."[43] It was, therefore, natural that the Spirit's work of providing divine testimony through inspiring Scripture would come to be associated with the Spirit's work of testifying to the person and work of the Son. This important connection will be explored in later chapters of this book.

The Personhood of the Paraclete

John's portrayal of the Holy Spirit as the Paraclete, tasked with providing divine testimony to the person and work of Jesus, had significant implications for developing conceptions of the Spirit's personhood. While it would be anachronistic to claim that John understood the Holy Spirit to

41. Brown, *Spirit in the Writings of John*, 251: "This question is not even answered obliquely in the text." Morgan-Wynne (*Holy Spirit*, 34) speculates that the implication appears to be that the Spirit would testify through the witness of the disciples.

42. McConnell, *Divine Testimony*, 174.

43. McConnell, *Divine Testimony*, 176.

be a distinct divine person in the sense of Nicene Christianity, there is nevertheless a sense in which the image of the Spirit as Paraclete conveys a more personal understanding of the Spirit than do other common images of the Spirit, such as wind, fire, a cloud, or a dove.[44] After all, this Paraclete is capable of being known (John 14:17), teaches the disciples (John 14:26), testifies on behalf of Jesus (John 15:26), convicts the world (John 16:8), and speaks what he hears (John 16:13). All of these verbs would seem to require a personal agent as their subject. Likewise, the images of the Spirit as a legal advocate or a broker of patronage communicate a clear sense of personhood. We must be careful, though, not to press this emerging sense of the Spirit's personhood too far. It is certainly possible, for instance, for literary personification to result in personal verbs being applied to nonpersonal subjects.[45] Nor should we assume personhood to imply divinity or distinction from the Father and the Son (see further the next section of this chapter).[46] Clearly, more definition will be required to flesh out an understanding of the Spirit as a distinct divine person.

Further caution is warranted. In their enthusiasm to demonstrate how John portrays the Spirit in personal terms, many exegetes and theologians have appealed to grammatical arguments. Typical is the claim of commentator Andrew Lincoln, who argues that in John 15:26 the Paraclete is "more clearly seen as a personal agent, since despite the neuter pronoun for the Spirit . . . the pronoun that is the subject of the main clause is nominative masculine."[47] This argument has been refuted by Daniel Wallace, who pointed out that the antecedent of the masculine pronoun is not "Spirit" but "Paraclete," which is grammatically masculine.[48] The fact that "Paraclete" is grammatically masculine is, likewise, irrelevant for constructing the Spirit's personhood or gender.[49] Likewise, some scholars have taken the use of the masculine participle in 1 John 5:7, which is followed by the neuter nouns "Spirit," "water," and "blood," to demonstrate

44. Kärkkäinen, *Pneumatology*, 15.

45. Wallace, "Greek Grammar," 124 n. 93 points to Sir 39:28 as an example of wind being personified.

46. Wallace, "Greek Grammar," 124.

47. Lincoln, *John*, 411–12. See also Barrett, *John*, 482; Brown, *Spirit in the Writings of John*, 201; Burge, *Anointed Community*, 142–43. For a history of this line of argument, see Wallace, "Greek Grammar," 100–104.

48. Wallace, "Greek Grammar," 104–8. To use technical language, "Spirit" is appositional to "Paraclete" and is therefore irrelevant for the gender of the pronoun.

49. Wallace, "Greek Grammar," 111–12.

the personhood of the Spirit.[50] Again, however, Wallace demonstrates that there are other reasons that can explain this shift in gender.[51] In sum, Wallace declares that because "none of the gender shift passages clearly helps establish the personality of the Holy Spirit," he recommends this argument "be excised from our theological textbooks."[52]

In the final accounting, our best way of understanding the presentation of the personality of the Spirit in the Johannine literature is to bear in mind the oneness of the Spirit and Christ. We see this, to take just one instance, in the reference to the Spirit as "another" Paraclete (John 14:16). Given that Jesus is the "other" Paraclete in view, this passage further underscores the close relationship between Jesus and the Spirit. In drawing this parallel, "the Spirit has taken on a fuller or more precise character—the character of Jesus."[53] On the one hand, the personality of the Spirit has been emphasized on account of Christ's personality being applied to the Spirit; on the other, though, it is not clear the extent to which the Spirit's personhood is distinct from that of the Son. Indeed, this is a further instance of the aforementioned phenomenon of Spirit Christology. Noting the intimate union of Christ and the Spirit in the Johannine writings, Burge reflects that "the Spirit is not a power impulsively in Jesus but an attribute of his own person."[54] In sum, therefore, we should on the whole be careful not to press the personhood of the Spirit too far in these passages, even as we admit that the image of the Spirit as Paraclete played an important role in the initiation and further development of reflection on the Spirit's distinct personhood over subsequent centuries.

The Old Testament Roots of the Paraclete

The Johannine portrayal of the Paraclete has its roots in the late Old Testament and intertestamental Jewish writings. Specifically, Jewish angelology offers a powerful precedent for the Paraclete and the Paraclete's forensic

---

50. For examples, see Wallace, "Greek Grammar," 118.

51. Wallace, "Greek Grammar," 119–20. Wallace emphasizes that the personal character of the "witnessing" in the passage, which in Jewish culture would have been exclusively carried out by males, is responsible for the shift.

52. Wallace, "Greek Grammar," 120.

53. Dunn, *Jesus and the Spirit*, 351.

54. Burge, *Anointed Community*, 87. Thus, the personalization of the Spirit has more to do with this union with Christ than with any Jewish angelic precedent (ibid.).

work. As Raymond Brown has described, the Jewish imagination conceived of angels (often called "spirits") at the heavenly court, and one angel in particular who "zealously protected God's interests on earth, rooting out evil."[55] This angel functioned as an advocate, then, clearly connecting to the Johannine depiction of the role of the Paraclete. As later Judaism embraced more of a dualistic worldview, Brown argues, this figure bifurcated into a "good" angel who is a heavenly witness for God and his people and a "bad" angel, Satan, the tempter.[56] In fact, at Qumran, the "Spirit of Truth" leads the community, dwells within human beings, and unites them with the truth, just as in the Gospel of John.[57] This image of the Paraclete as an angelic advocate was then combined with Jewish notions of the Spirit of God coming upon the prophets and the personified figure of Wisdom to bolster John's depiction of the Spirit's teaching ministry.[58] In sum, then, the Johannine portrayal of the Paraclete is deeply indebted to late Jewish ideas, with the notion of the Paraclete as Advocate standing in direct continuity with the tradition of Jewish angelology.

The significance of this is threefold. First, even at this early stage, Christian theologizing on the person and work of the Spirit was carried out in light of careful reflection on the Scriptures, including what we would now call apocryphal and intertestamental literature. This process of reflecting on the Scriptures, as we will see, will continue to drive pneumatological development in subsequent centuries even after Christianity and Judaism came to identify as distinct religious communities. Second, the background of Jewish angelology should caution us against assuming that portrayals of the Spirit as personal also intend to communicate that the Spirit is divine, even if John's reworking of these traditions set up a movement in this direction. After all, Jewish angelology held that these angels were created beings, and therefore not the deity itself.[59] Assuming a progressive development of

55. Brown, *John XIII–XXI*, 1138, with reference to Job 1:6–12; Zech 3:1–5. See also Lincoln, *John*, 393.

56. Brown, *John XIII–XXI*, 1138, with reference to Dan 10:13; Job 16:19, 19:25–27, 33:23; Wis 1:7–9; Jub. 1.19–24.

57. Brown, *John XIII–XXI*, 1138, with reference to 1QS III, 6–7; 1QS IV, 23–24; cf. T.Jud. 20:1–5.

58. Brown, *John XIII–XXI*, 1139, with reference to Sir 24:12, 26–27, 33. For a full history of scholarly approaches to the relevant background for the Paraclete, see further Burge, *Anointed Community*, 10–31.

59. On the angelic nature of the Spirit in first-century Judaism, with reference to parallels in contemporary Greco-Roman literature, see Levison, *Spirit in First-Century*

the understanding of the person and work of the Spirit, it seems that John's own pneumatology was likely closer to that of his Qumran contemporaries than that of the fourth-century church fathers. Third, this particular pneumatological trajectory, often referred to as angelomorphic pneumatology in the literature, continued to exert enormous influence in the pre-Nicene period even as some church fathers began constructing a different understanding of the Spirit as a distinct divine person.[60]

Still, the significance of John's portrayal of the Spirit as an advocate who is the source of divine testimony cannot be understated. Irrespective of the Jewish angelic background for the concept, John's Paraclete established within the Christian tradition a link between the Holy Spirit and divine testimony, a link that would be further developed and clarified by subsequent Christian writers.[61] Interestingly, it would be a very different set of Old Testament passages, read through the lens of a very different interpretive method, that would be used to fill out the picture of the Spirit's testifying work.

Elsewhere in the New Testament

This chapter has argued that the Johannine depiction of the Paraclete was the most important New Testament portrayal of the Spirit in terms of emerging notions of the Spirit's personhood and divine testimony. Briefly, however, we may survey some of the other New Testament texts that I believe were instrumental in later Christian reflection on the Spirit's provision of divine testimony. In this section, we will examine two further New Testament passages, 1 Cor 2:10–12 and Heb 10:15–17, with respect to this issue of the Spirit's divine testimony.[62]

Judaism, 25–54. The angelic spirit seems to function to preserve God's distance from unsavory scenes, such as the account of Balaam's oracles (Num 22–24).

60. On the lasting influence of angelomorphic pneumatology in the early church, see Bucur, *Angelomorphic Pneumatology*. As defined by Bucur (*Angelomorphic Pneumatology*, xxvi), the term "angelomorphic" "signals the use of angelic *characteristics* in descriptions of God or humans, while not necessarily implying that either are angels *stricto sensu*" (italics original).

61. On the extensive influence of the Gospel of John in the early church, see Hill, *Johannine Corpus*.

62. This section builds upon my discussion in Hughes, *Trinitarian Testimony*, 87–94.

1 Corinthians 2:10–12

A complete summary of Pauline pneumatology is beyond the scope of this chapter, although I will again note my sense that, over time, Paul moves in the direction of a more personal understanding of the Spirit even as he continues to on occasion present a more impersonal view.[63] In the early chapters of his first letter to the church in Corinth, Paul is expounding upon the theme of the wisdom of God. Having just contrasted the wisdom of God with the wisdom of this world (1 Cor 2:6–9), Paul now turns to consider how the Spirit mediates God's wisdom. Specifically, God has "revealed" to the apostles and other teachers, through the Spirit, his previously secret and hidden plan of salvation (1 Cor 2:10a).[64] The Spirit is the right agent to reveal these supernatural secrets, Paul writes, because "the Spirit searches everything, even the depths of God" (1 Cor 2:10b); after all, only the Spirit of God can understand the things of God (1 Cor 2:11). The Spirit, Paul explains, helps believers to understand the nature of their salvation (1 Cor 2:12).[65] Thus, according to Paul, the role of the Spirit is to take what the Spirit alone knows about God and make it known to believers.[66] Though the language of testimony is not explicitly employed in this passage, the Spirit's act of "revealing" the nature of God's gift of salvation in Christ may be seen as parallel to the Spirit's work of testifying to the person and work of Christ.

Indeed, this understanding of the Spirit's work can help us make sense of Paul's statement in 1 Cor 12:3 that "no one can say 'Jesus is Lord' except by the Holy Spirit." It is, therefore, the Spirit and not the individual believer making this confession.[67] Because the Spirit is here identified as the means by which Jesus' true nature is revealed, enabling believers to correctly confess the person and work of Christ, this would appear to be in line with the notion that only the Spirit knows the things of God and can reveal them to

63. For a summary of Pauline pneumatology, see Fee, *God's Empowering Presence*; Thiselton, *Holy Spirit*, 70–94.

64. The language of "revelation" is just one of many signals that an apocalyptic worldview is running through this passage; see Collins, *First Corinthians*, 124–26.

65. The pronoun "we" throughout 1 Cor 2:6–13 poses some interpretive challenges; my interpretation of this passage reflects Ciampa and Rosner, *First Letter to the Corinthians*, 121–34.

66. This argument draws on the logic of Platonism, which held that "like is known only by like"; as such, God's Spirit is required to link God and humanity and make God known to human beings; see Fee, *First Corinthians*, 110; Collins, *First Corinthians*, 133.

67. Barrett, *First Epistle to the Corinthians*, 281.

believers.[68] In both John and Paul, therefore, the Spirit communicates vital information about Christ to his followers.

Hebrews 10:15–17

The Letter to the Hebrews is unique in the New Testament insofar as it presents the Spirit as speaking the words of the Old Testament in at least three instances.[69] Among these passages, Heb 10:15–17 stands out as particularly interesting with respect to the theme of the Spirit and divine testimony. In this portion of the epistle (Heb 10:11–18), the author is arguing that the sacrifice of Jesus, the perfect high priest, established God's promised new covenant. As evidence, the author appeals to the Holy Spirit, who "testifies to us" with a form of the words of Jer 31:33–34 as the summation of the aforementioned new covenant.[70] What is uniquely fascinating about this text is that not only is the Spirit speaking through the words of Scripture, but the Spirit, as in John, is engaged in the work of providing testimony. While the Spirit is not testifying to or about God in this particular instance, there is a thematic coherence at work that is suggestive of the extent to which the Spirit came to be linked with the idea of testimony by the writers of the New Testament.

What will be of particular interest for tracing the rise of significant themes in early Christian pneumatology is how the Spirit, Scripture, and testimony are brought into conjunction in this passage. Thus, the form of the Spirit's testimony, which was not explicitly specified in John, has here been identified as occurring through the words of the Old Testament. The precise nature of how the Spirit testifies through Scripture, however, is still opaque; whereas the Jeremiah text is said to be spoken by "the LORD," or YHWH, Hebrews attributes it instead to the Spirit. It is therefore unclear whether we are to understand the Spirit as inspiring the prophet to record these words of YHWH or if we are to see the Spirit as standing in for YHWH in some capacity. Looking at the other Old Testament passages attributed to the Spirit in Hebrews, the Spirit simply seems to be re-presenting the words of Scripture to the audience of the epistle (Heb 3:7–11) or interpreting the true significance of Scripture in a christological light (Heb 9:6–10);

68. Fee, *First Corinthians*, 582.

69. See further Emmrich, "*Pneuma* in Hebrews," 55–56; for more on the pneumatology of Hebrews more generally, see Thiselton, *Holy Spirit*, 153–56.

70. On the form of this citation, see Emmrich, "*Pneuma* in Hebrews," 60–63.

the testimony motif does not appear to be in view, unlike the case of Heb 10:15–17.[71] Even so, this notion of the Spirit speaking through the Old Testament text is significant. As Martin Emmrich has concluded, at the time this epistle was written, the Spirit's prophetic activity was mostly judged to have taken place in the distant past; in Hebrews, however, it is in the present day that the Spirit functions as an eschatological, "prophetic orator" to the community.[72] As we will see, the belief in the Spirit's inspiration of the Old Testament and, moreover, the Spirit's present re-presentation or interpretation of the Scriptures would continue to influence the pneumatological trajectory that we will examine over the course of this book.

Conclusion

As argued in this chapter, the first generation of Christians identified themselves as the people who had experienced the risen and exalted Christ through the Holy Spirit. Over time, these first Christians would have sought to explain their experience and relate it to other aspects of their beliefs and practices. In particular, as a sect of Second Temple Judaism, it would have been natural for these first Christians to reflect critically upon the Jewish Scriptures to construct their understanding of this Holy Spirit; it was the Old Testament, therefore, to which the Christians turned. Among the wide range of such articulations of the Spirit found in the New Testament, we focused upon the Johannine presentation of the Paraclete as being particularly significant insofar as it set forth the most personal portrayal of the Spirit in the New Testament. Drawing primarily upon the tradition of Jewish angelology and the Greco-Roman rhetorical category of divine testimony, John identified an essential function of the Spirit as providing testimony to the true nature of Jesus' person and work. Though this view of the Spirit is most thoroughly presented in the Johannine writings, some parallel ideas may be found elsewhere in the New Testament, namely 1 Corinthians and Hebrews, establishing a broad basis for this idea to take root in the minds of later generations of Christians.

71. See again Emmrich, "*Pneuma* in Hebrews," 56–60, 63–66. According to Bates (*Birth*, 163–65), the unidentified speaker of Ps 45:6–7 at Heb 1:8–9 is likely the Holy Spirit, but this reading can only be sustained by reading backwards from how later church fathers interpreted this passage.

72. Emmrich, "*Pneuma* in Hebrews," 66–68; on the Jewish belief that the Spirit had "ceased" with the final biblical prophets, Emmrich points to 1 Macc 4:46, 9:27, 14:41; Josephus, *Ag. Ap.* 1.41.

One popular line of argument holds that with the passing of the first generation of Christians, the pneumatic and charismatic character of early Christianity declined. In the Pauline churches, the gifts of the Spirit are often said to have diminished after Paul's death. After all, even within Paul's lifetime, the actual lived experience of a charismatic community proved deeply problematic.[73] Indeed, assuming a later date for the Pastoral Epistles, these texts could be read to indicate that the initial power of the experience of Christ through the Spirit had faded, with church order, ritual, and tradition instead serving as the organizing principles of the communities.[74] Likewise, while a vital experience of the Spirit seems to have lasted longer in the Johannine community than in the Pauline churches, even here it is claimed that initial charismatic enthusiasm gave way to a more circumscribed role for the Spirit—the so-called "Johannine adjustment" found in 1 John. The author of this epistle, suspicious of prophetic activity, therefore limits the work of the Spirit to preserving tradition; the ability of the Spirit to provide fresh revelation along the lines of John 16:12–13 seems to have been ruled out of bounds.[75]

While these points of evidence do represent a significant shift from the first generation, it is nevertheless the case that Christians of the second generation and beyond continued to believe in a living and active Spirit, not just along the lines suggested in 1 John but also through the continued experience of miracles and other gifts of the Spirit.[76] In any event, another major change with enormous implications for the Christian faith more generally and for views of the Holy Spirit more particularly was taking place: the construction of Christianity as a religion increasingly distinct from Judaism, which is the subject of our next chapter.

Thus, looking at the finished mosaic of the Holy Spirit that serves as the metaphor for the process of theological development explored in this book, we first marvel at how the tiles have managed to adhere to the wall for so many centuries. This strong and lasting adhesive represents the experience of the Spirit, and therefore we can date the first mixing of

73. Dunn, *Jesus and the Spirit*, 266–71; cf. 1 Cor 12–14.

74. Dunn, *Jesus and the Spirit*, 349. Dunn punts on the exact reason for this decline, though he argues that in any event "the only way the author of the Pastorals felt able to maintain Christianity was by formalization of faith and institutionalization of church" (ibid.). For a balanced approach to the question of the authorship and therefore dating of the Pastorals, see Gorman, *Apostle of the Crucified Lord*, 107–109, 612–15.

75. Burge, *Anointed Community*, 219–20; cf. Morgan-Wynne, *Holy Spirit*, 103.

76. Skarsaune, *Shadow*, 340; Morgan-Wynne, *Holy Spirit*.

this adhesive as far back as that first Pentecost. Turning to the tiles of the mosaic itself, among the tiles crafted by the first generation of Christians, our eyes are struck by one particularly important tile, crafted by John the Evangelist, representing the Spirit's work in providing divine testimony. Like all the other tiles, it was crafted from the material of Old Testament interpretation and it adheres to the wall via the experience of the Spirit. This tile, if you look at it in just the right light, gives off a glimmer suggesting that this tile in fact introduces a further theme in the mosaic, that of the Spirit's personhood. Taking in the whole mosaic, it appears that this tile was unusually important in setting the mosaic's subsequent patterns, with some of the most visually stunning portions of the mosaic branching out from it in new and surprising ways.

CHAPTER 3

The Spirit and Christian Identity

I n the year 70 CE, the Romans destroyed the Second Temple in Jerusalem, marking the end of both the period scholars refer to as Second Temple Judaism and what we might call the "first generation" of emergent Christianity. Up until this point, Christianity was best understood not as a distinct religion but as a sect within the broader milieu of Second Temple Judaism. The events of 70 CE, though, would be a major inflection point, having profound implications for the religious landscape of antiquity. For its part, Judaism survived the destruction of the Temple and reorganized in what we call the rabbinic period, centering itself on Torah in lieu of temple. As gentiles came to outnumber Jews in the early church, it was only inevitable that Christians began to no longer identify themselves as part of a messianic sect of Judaism but rather as comprising a distinct entity defined in many respects by its opposition to Judaism. Over the next one hundred years, Christianity would come to take on a number of its enduring features with respect to its theology, worship, and organization.[1]

Traditionally, scholars and historians have used the term "the parting of the ways" to describe the separation of Christianity from Judaism in the first centuries of the Common Era. The problem with this view, however, is that it presupposes that in this early period there would have been distinct, readily identifiable entities that we could label "Judaism" or "Christianity." The reality is much more complex, with the boundaries between these groups fluid and continually contested over the course of many centuries. To use the imagery of James Dunn, perhaps a more satisfying image is that of "a landscape of moor or hillside crisscrossed by several or many

---

1. For an overview of this process, see Dunn, *Neither Jew nor Greek*, 1–26. As Dunn (ibid.,12) points out, the term "Christianity" was first used in extant writings by Ignatius of Antioch in the 110s CE.

paths, whose directions are not always clear and which ramblers or fell-walkers may follow without a clear sense of where they are headed."[2] It is better, therefore, to speak of a process of mutual self-definition, in which groups that were originally only somewhat socially differentiated came to identify themselves as distinct religious communities.[3] After all, insofar as Christianity began as an enthusiastic, messianic sect within Judaism, it would be a long and messy process for Christians to fashion an identity that would both stand in continuity with the Scriptures and worldview they had received on account of their Jewish heritage and demonstrate discontinuity with emerging rabbinic Judaism, reflecting the increasing gentile composition of the church.

Within this broader process of constructing a distinctively Christian identity, we are particularly interested in how the Christian understanding of the Spirit was shaped by this struggle with Judaism. As we will see in this chapter, one of the most important developments in the narrative of how the Spirit came to be identified as a distinct divine person was the process by which the Spirit came to be seen as fully, and even exclusively, as belonging to the Christians. In order to explore this theme in more detail, we need to examine the pneumatological perspectives of two important early Christian texts: the pseudonymous Epistle of Barnabas and Justin Martyr's *Dialogue with Trypho*.

The Epistle of Barnabas

The Epistle of Barnabas, traditionally associated with the second-generation collection of Christian writings known as the Apostolic Fathers, is an unusual and fascinating piece of early Christian literature. For one thing, we know nothing of its author or editor (besides that it was almost certainly not the apostle Barnabas), and its date of composition and provenance are fiercely debated.[4] Despite these mysteries, the argument of the epistle is straightforward, promoting a Christian understanding of the "perfect knowledge" of life, righteousness, and love, in light of a correct interpretation of the Old

2. Dunn, *Neither Jew nor Greek*, 16.

3. For this view, see besides Dunn the seminal works of Boyarin, *Border Lines*; Lieu, *Image and Reality*.

4. Following Jefford (*Apostolic Fathers*, 7–9) and Carleton Paget (*Barnabas*, 9–42), I hold to the theory that places the text's final composition in the years 96–100 CE in or around the city of Alexandria in Egypt.

Testament.[5] Unfortunately, the epistle is perhaps best known for its harsh anti-Jewish polemic, which can be exceedingly uncomfortable to modern ears in light of many centuries of subsequent anti-Semitism. Still, this text has a lot to tell us about the early process of Christian self-differentiation, particularly with respect to emerging Christian views of the Spirit. Interestingly, scholarship has largely ignored the epistle's contributions to pneumatology.[6] As we will see, however, the epistle's author seeks to creatively link his audience's present experience of the Spirit with claims about how this Spirit was at work even in Old Testament times, thereby creating both a distinct, separate identity for his community as it sought to define itself in opposition to developing rabbinic Judaism and shape an explicitly Christian identity based on the possession of the Spirit.

The Christian Work of the Spirit in the Old Testament

Before we consider the innovative way in which the epistle claims both Old Testament heroes and the Spirit for Christianity, we need to broaden our perspective on its overall argument. In the context of the aforementioned process of early Christian self-definition, the epistle captures a moment in time in which Judaism was seen as an increasingly distinct threat and competitor to what was coming to be identified as a distinctively Christian religious movement. The author of Barnabas is, therefore, preoccupied with demonstrating the superiority of emergent Christianity over Judaism.[7] In particular, as Reidar Hvalvik has demonstrated, the author of the epistle is particularly concerned that his audience not abandon the Christian faith for Judaism, and accordingly one of his primary strategies in this writing "is to capture the treasures of Judaism: their Scripture and their covenant."[8]

---

5. Barn. 1.5–6; see further Jefford, *Apostolic Fathers*, 9–10. Translations of the Epistle of Barnabas are taken from Holmes, *Apostolic Fathers*.

6. For instance, Thiselton (*Holy Spirit*, 168) simply notes how the epistle emphasizes the Spirit's roles in preparing people for the gospel and in baptism. Even in recent monographs on Barnabas, the Spirit recedes into the distance; for example, Hvalvik (*Struggle*, 104), devotes only a single paragraph to the topic of the epistle's pneumatology, emphasizing the Spirit's prophetic inspiration of Scripture.

7. Hvalvik, *Struggle*, 99; see also Carleton Paget, *Barnabas*, 69: the author "seeks to give the Christian community for whom he is writing a clear identity over against the majority Jewish community."

8. Hvalvik, *Struggle*, 329.

This significant point can be unpacked in more detail before we see how the Spirit specifically fits into this process.

With respect to the struggle for Scripture, the epistle reveals a tension in the early church: despite the need to clarify and defend the Christian religion with respect to Judaism, Christianity nevertheless made its claims with reference to the Jewish Scriptures. Jews, of course, continued to also read their Scriptures and undoubtedly believed the sacred texts rightly belonged to them. The solution of Barnabas was to argue that the Scriptures belonged to the Christians and not the Jews because the Jews had from the beginning misunderstood and failed to obey these Scriptures. For the author of Barnabas, all of Scripture points to Christ and Christianity.[9] As for the struggle for the covenant, given that the author of the epistle is concerned to demonstrate the superiority of Christianity over Judaism, he argues that God's covenant was originally offered to the Jews, in the form of commandments, but the Jews rejected the Sinai covenant at the time of the golden calf incident (cf. Exod 32:1–10); with the coming of Christ, the covenant was then offered to the Christians, in the form of forgiveness (Barn. 14.1–9).[10] Interestingly, this argument that the Jews lost the covenant at Sinai was not picked up by later Christian writers, who were perhaps not convinced by it on account of its neglect to mention the fact that God gave the Jews new tablets of the covenant at Sinai (a detail that Barnabas conveniently glosses over). In any event, for Barnabas, the golden calf episode cast the fate of the Jews, who failed to understand and obey God's commandments from the first (Barn. 4.8, 10.12).[11] Both the Scriptures and the covenant, therefore, were the exclusive property of the Christians, and so, the author of the epistle concludes, his wavering audience should not abandon Christianity for Judaism.

This brings us, then, to the Spirit, for these claims are further reflected in how Barnabas views the work of the Spirit in the period before the coming of Christ. The author of the epistle focuses on three examples of Old Testament saints who, he claims, looked forward to Christ by means of the Spirit, thereby claiming even the great heroes of the Jewish faith for

9. Hvalvik, *Struggle*, 132–33: "Everything found in the history of the Jews is directly related to Christ and his people, and thus has no independent value or meaning as part of their history"; as such, "the idea of salvation-historical epochs—where Old Testament persons, events and institutions are thought to have a preliminary meaning and independent significance—is not found in *Barnabas*."

10. Hvalvik, *Struggle*, 153.

11. Hvalvik, *Struggle*, 154.

Christianity. Of course, contemporaneous writings demonstrate that Barnabas had ample precedent for the belief that the Old Testament saints looked forward to Christ. For example, the Johannine Jesus remarks, "Your ancestor Abraham rejoiced that he would see my day; he saw it and was glad" (John 8:56). The most sustained argument of this nature is found in Heb 11; after commending the faith of various Old Testament saints, the writer of that epistle concludes, "All of these died in faith without having received the promises, but from a distance they saw and greeted them" (Heb 11:13). In both John and Hebrews, there is the notion that these figures somehow "saw" the fulfillment of the promises of God in Christ.[12] Barnabas, however, carries this line of argument forward by clarifying and developing how this "seeing" occurred: *by the Spirit*.[13]

The first example that demonstrates this point is Abraham (Barn. 9.7–8). Here Barnabas tells us that "Abraham, who first instituted circumcision, looked forward in the [S]pirit to Jesus when he circumcised, having received the teaching of the three letters."[14] Interestingly, the verb translated "looked forward" in this passage occurs only once in the New Testament (Heb 11:40), with God as the subject and with a much different nuance;[15] it is in that same chapter of Hebrews, of course, that we find the aforementioned reference to Abraham and others who looked forward to God's fulfillment of his promises in Christ (Heb 11:13). Though both references to Abraham highlight this future-looking aspect of his faith, the account of Abraham in Barnabas is nevertheless considerably different from what is found in Heb 11:8–19. In Hebrews, Abraham is praised

12. That Jesus fulfilled the promises of the Old Testament is of course a consistent and important theme across the New Testament; see, e.g., Matt 5:17–18; Luke 24:27; John 5:39, 46; 2 Cor 1:20. On the transformation of Old Testament ideas of the prophets "seeing" God to apply to Christ, see John 12:41, with reference to Isa 6:1–13.

13. This chapter thus attempts to go beyond Thiselton (*Holy Spirit*, 164), who observed that in Barnabas "the author explicitly associates the inspiration of the Holy Spirit with Abraham, Moses, and other Old Testament figures." This view of the Spirit's inspiration could just as equally apply to an analysis of John or Hebrews; here we seek to identify what is *distinct* about the presentation of Barnabas. To clarify, this is not to say that the author of Barnabas had knowledge of John or Hebrews; the point is simply that these other early Christian texts make for a useful comparison with Barnabas.

14. Oddly, Holmes' translation (*Apostolic Fathers*, 407) does not capitalize "spirit" in "spirit of the Lord" here or at Barn. 9.2, although he does at Barn. 6.14.

15. The verb here is *problepō*. Luke Timothy Johnson (*Hebrews*, 309) notes that the emphasis is on how "the promise [of what God has 'prepared'] remains for the hearers" of Hebrews.

for the faith by which he went to live in the promised land (Heb 11:9) and offered Isaac on the altar (Heb 11:17–19). Abraham's hope is there described in vague and general terms: "he looked forward to the city that has foundations, whose architect and builder is God" (Heb 11:10).[16] While superficially more specific in its explicit reference to Christ, the claim in John 8:56 that Abraham "rejoiced that he would see my day" is similarly general with respect to means and specific details.[17] The contrast between Hebrews and Barnabas is illuminative. Going beyond what either Hebrews or John had described, Barnabas not only tells us that Abraham looked forward to Jesus (Barn. 9.7) but also goes on to explicate the precise manner in which Abraham "saw" Jesus: if the number of men Abraham circumcised, 318, is rewritten as *nomina sacra* both the person of Jesus and his death on the cross are revealed (Barn. 9.8).[18] As Hvalvik points out, though the author of Barnabas "was not able to hide the fact that Abraham really circumcised," it does not in the author's mind "legitimate the Jewish practice of carnal circumcision," because Abraham's circumcision was in fact a "prophetic act."[19] Most importantly for our purposes, though, is the note that Abraham did this prophetic action "in the [S]pirit" (Barn. 9.7). It is the Spirit, then, who is the source of this revelation.

A second example of this theme is found in the epistle's account of Moses (Barn. 12.2–7). Here the author of the epistle retells the story of the Israelites' victory over the Amalekites in Exod 17:8–13, which required Moses to keep his hands outstretched until Israel secured the victory. The Exodus account gives no explicit reason for why this particular action was required, but Barnabas fills in the gaps by suggesting that the image of Moses with his arms outstretched was in fact a prefiguration of the cross of Christ. In the same way, Moses "makes a symbol of Jesus" by lifting up a bronze serpent for the salvation of the people (Barn. 12.5–7; cf. Num

16. On this passage, see Johnson, *Hebrews*, 288–92.

17. By Jesus' "day," he likely means "the last day," that is, the day of resurrection; cf. Michaels, *John*, 532: "Abraham, consequently, in anticipating and then experiencing (in his own fashion) the resurrection, 'saw Jesus' day' and became the beneficiary of eternal life."

18. A *nomen sacrum* is a contraction of a sacred word made by Christian scribes that frequently appears in ancient biblical manuscripts; see further Metzger and Ehrman, *Text of the New Testament*, 23–24. The idea in Barn. 9.7–8 depends on the ancient correspondence between Greek letters of the alphabet and specific numbers; see further the discussion in Holmes, *Apostolic Fathers*, 409.

19. Hvalvik, *Struggle*, 126.

21:4–8; John 3:14–15) and reveals Jesus "by a symbol" through the similarly named Joshua (Barn. 12.8–10; cf. Exod 17:14). Throughout, the author of Barnabas is concerned to make the point that, with respect to Christ, "all things are in him and for him" (Barn. 12.7), and thus christological interpretation is necessary to correctly understand Scripture.[20] But what is perhaps most significant about how Barnabas uses Scripture here is the actual result of his typological interpretation.[21] For the author of Barnabas, God revealed everything pertaining to Christ in advance. And just as Abraham "saw" Christ clearly in his own day, so too Moses had explicit understanding of Jesus, with Barnabas noting that "Moses himself made one [carved image, that is, the bronze serpent] in order to show them a symbol of Jesus" (Barn. 12.6). But how? Again, the epistle assigns this role to the Spirit, recounting how "the Spirit says to the heart of Moses that he should make a symbol" (Barn. 12.2). Just as with Abraham, therefore, the Spirit is the source of the prophetic revelation of Christ to Moses. And whereas the author of Hebrews also claims that Moses "considered abuse suffered for the Christ to be greater wealth than the treasures of Egypt, for he was looking ahead to the reward" (Heb 11:26),[22] Barnabas again fills in the mechanism by which Moses looked forward to Christ: the Spirit.

A third instance of an Old Testament saint looking forward to Christ is Jacob (Barn. 13.4–6). In the story of Jacob blessing the sons of Joseph (Gen 48:1–20), Jacob gives the greater blessing to Ephraim despite the fact that Manasseh is Joseph's firstborn. The reason given in the Genesis account is that Jacob foresaw that Ephraim would become a greater nation than Manasseh (Gen 48:19). The author of Barnabas reads this scene typologically, exhorting his audience to "observe how by these means he has ordained that this people should be first, and heir of the covenant" (Barn. 13.6). Of course, by "this people" he means the Christians, a theme that Barnabas has emphasized starting in Barn. 13.1. The two peoples that Barnabas envisions in this chapter are the Jews and the Christians, with the latter group apparently understood to consist exclusively of gentiles.[23] Again, the

20. Hvalvik, *Struggle*, 191.

21. Hvalvik, *Struggle*, 117: "In Barnabas' view this [typological] interpretation is not a secondary reading of the text, but an unveiling of the *original* significance of what Moses did" (italics original).

22. Cf. Johnson, *Hebrews*, 298–301.

23. Barn. 13.7 seems to leave no room for Jewish Christians: "Behold, I have established you, Abraham, as the father of the nations who believe in God without being circumcised." See further Hvalvik, *Struggle*, 146–48.

thrust of the argument is clear: the Christians are superior to the Jews, with yet another Old Testament saint summoned as a witness to this fact—in this case, no less a witness than Jacob, the man from whom the people of Israel took their name. The manner in which Jacob was claimed for the Christians parallels the other examples we have just examined; Jacob, we are told, "saw in the Spirit a symbol of the people to come" (Barn. 13.5). Thus, for a third time, we observe that the means by which these patriarchs looked forward to Christ and his church was the Spirit.

By claiming that Abraham, Jacob, and Moses, three of the most important figures in the history of the people of Israel, had foreknowledge of Christ and the salvation he would bring, the author of the epistle in effect claims them as Christians.[24] This is, and no doubt was at the time, an audacious claim.

What the preceding analysis has shown is that Barnabas consistently credits the Spirit as the actor through whom (or, perhaps more precisely at this point, "through which," but see below) these Old Testament saints foresaw Christ. The Spirit, far from being a tangential element in the author of the epistle's thought, is in fact the very means by which Christ was made known in the past.

Additionally, and significantly for the argument of this book, Barnabas argues not only that the Spirit inspired others to look forward to Christ but also that the Spirit himself, in some manner that can only be described as personal, looked forward to Christ. In Barn. 6.14, the Spirit "foresaw" those whose stony hearts the Lord would replace with hearts of flesh. Interestingly, the verb used here of the Spirit is the same as was used with Abraham, establishing that in some sense the Spirit looked forward to the coming of Christ and the birth of the church in the same way that Abraham and the other Old Testament saints had done.[25] Even so, lest we read back later developments into this text, we should be careful not to assume too developed of a sense of distinct personhood in this depiction of the Spirit. After all, the Spirit is in Barn. 6.14 and 9.2 referred to as "the Spirit of the Lord." As argued in the previous chapter of this book, this phrase signals the presence of a Spirit Christology in which there is considerable overlap of the function and even the identity of the Son

---

24. As is the case in Hebrews; see further Johnson, *Hebrews*, 293: "the author here effectively makes the structure and goal of the patriarchs' faith the same as the Christians.'"

25. See Hvalvik, *Struggle*, 104, with reference to the Spirit's prophetic inspiration of Scripture. The verb here is (again) *problepō*.

and the Spirit; in this usage we may hear echoes, for instance, of Paul's description of the Spirit as the "Spirit of Christ" (Rom 8:9; Phil 1:19) or of the Johannine portrayal of the oneness of the Spirit and Christ. Barnabas does not, therefore, provide anything that would contribute to a clearer picture of the Spirit's distinct personhood. Still, this Christianization of the Spirit, however defined, would have implications for the construction of Christian self-identity, as we will continue to explore in Barnabas and then in Justin Martyr.

The Experience of the Spirit

Having looked at the role of the Spirit in the period before the coming of Christ, we can now examine what the epistle says about the present experience of that same Spirit. For the author of Barnabas, the Spirit is living and active in the midst of the Christian community being addressed by the epistle, with the Spirit calling followers of Christ to lives of obedience. Here we will briefly explore how the community to which Barnabas was written experienced the Spirit through Scripture and sacrament before demonstrating the significance of how the author of Barnabas connects the past and present work of the Holy Spirit to set forth a distinctly Christian vision of the Holy Spirit.

One way in which the community to which the epistle was addressed experienced the Spirit was through the Spirit's re-presentation of Scripture. We see this, for instance, in Barn. 9.2b–3, where the author refers to the Spirit as the one who "prophesies" to the community through the words of the Old Testament. Interestingly, whereas other Old Testament quotations are attributed to "the Lord" (Barn. 9.1–2a), in Barn. 9.2b–3 the Spirit is summoned as the divine orator who is re-presenting the words of the Old Testament to a present-day audience. As discussed in the previous chapter of this book, this is a relatively unique phenomenon among early Christian writings, with the only other examples found in the New Testament letter to the Hebrews.[26] Just as in Hebrews, Barn. 9.2b–3 appears to present the Spirit speaking in a manner that is both christological and eschatological. For

---

26. See again Heb 3:7–11, 9:6–10, 10:15–17. A separate phenomenon, in which the Holy Spirit speaks independent of any clear Old Testament text, should also be noted; see further Aune, *Prophecy*, 443 n. 38: "the formula 'thus says the (Holy) Spirit' (and variations) is clearly a prophetic speech formula in early Christianity." Aune cites Acts 21:11; Rev 2:7, 2:11, 2:17, 2:29, 3:6, 3:13, 3:22; Ign. *Phil.* 7.2 as examples.

example, the quotation in Barn. 9.2b, a catena of verses including Ps 34:12, Isa 50:10, and Exod 15:26, is christological insofar as it calls attention to Jesus as the "servant" of God. And not only this, but it is also eschatological insofar as it envisions future salvation as a reward for those who hear and heed the Lord's message. The call for an immediate response from the epistle's audience most closely resembles the function of the Spirit in Heb 3:7–11. The context of this passage, though, begins to establish where Barnabas goes beyond the depiction of the Spirit's work found in Hebrews. Broadly speaking, the author of the epistle is here arguing that the Christians, as opposed to the Jews, practice true circumcision (Barn. 9.1–9), which James Carleton Paget has argued likely "reflects a genuine fear on the part of [the author] that some Christians wished to be circumcised."[27] The Spirit is therefore functioning on the side of the Christians in Barnabas' construction of more firm boundary lines between Jews and Christians.

This issue is complicated, however, by other features of this passage. The Spirit is here identified as "the Spirit of the Lord," which as we noted above suggests some degree of a Spirit Christology operating in the background of the epistle; this is perhaps part of the reason why it is difficult to trace whether the Lord or the Spirit is meant to be understood as the speaker of the quotations in this passage that do not have an explicit speaker assigned. Still, perhaps the rough outlines of a pattern are beginning to emerge: "the Lord" is likely the speaker of those texts in which the Lord is clearly understood to be *himself* speaking in the first-person, whereas "the Spirit of the Lord" is speaking when the Spirit speaks in the first-person *about* the Lord.[28] This lack of clarity, though, contrasts with the more methodical approach to identifying the speakers of Old Testament texts that will be evident in later writers such as Justin Martyr and Irenaeus (see the next chapter of this book). In any event, in Barnabas as in Hebrews there seems to be the sense that the Spirit functions to call God's people to a deeper understanding of the christological and eschatological dimensions of Scripture.

A second way in which the community experienced the Spirit was through sacrament. Further going beyond what Hebrews explicitly states, the epistle argues that the reason that the Christian community can hear and obey God's words is that the Spirit has been poured out upon them. At the outset of the letter, the author writes, "Therefore I, who also am hoping to be

27. Carleton Paget, *Barnabas*, 149.

28. This nevertheless produces the unusual reading at Barn. 9.2b that the Spirit speaks of Christ as "my servant."

saved, congratulate myself all the more because among you I truly see that the Spirit has been poured out upon you from the riches of the Lord's fountain" (Barn. 1.3).[29] Thus, the author of the epistle claims to have first-hand evidence of the experience of the Spirit in this community, perhaps related to his observation of the community's possession of Christian character in the form of faith, hope, and love (Barn. 1.4).[30] The epistle seems to imply elsewhere that an individual's experience of the Spirit began with the sacrament of baptism, citing a sequence of Old Testament passages that cluster around images involving wood and water (Barn. 11.1–11).[31] As indicated throughout the epistle, for Barnabas, God revealed everything pertaining to Christ in advance, and baptism is no different: the epistle informs us that the Lord "took care to foreshadow the water and the cross" (Barn. 11.1). In concluding his analysis of this subject, the author of the epistle claims that those who enter the waters of baptism "rise up bearing fruit in our heart and with fear and hope in Jesus by the Spirit" (Barn. 11.11).[32] The Spirit is the agent at work in the waters of baptism, just as the Spirit is active in calling those whom the Spirit has prepared (Barn. 19.7). In light of the contrast that the author of the epistle is drawing between Christian and Jewish baptism (Barn. 11.1), the implication therefore seems to be that the Jews, lacking the baptism of the Spirit, are thereby unable to rightly understand the Scripture inspired by that same Spirit.[33] The full results of this logic about the transfer of the Spirit from the Jews to the Christians will be worked out in more detail by Justin Martyr, to whom we will next attend.

Thus, the epistle connects the same Spirit that illuminated the Old Testament saints about Christ with the Spirit that is now re-presenting Scripture to the community and continues to be poured out upon believers at baptism. The defining mark of Christians in the present age is in

---

29. The reference here is to Joel 2:23, making this an eschatological claim; as in the New Testament, Barnabas sees the present experience of the Spirit as evidence that the last days are at hand (Barn. 4.9), with the coming of the Lord (Barn. 21.3) and the day of judgment (Barn. 21.7) still future.

30. Morgan-Wynne, *Holy Spirit*, 111.

31. Skarsaune, *Proof from Prophecy*, 378–79, sees parallels between this passage and Justin, *Dial.* 86, and suggests this was drawn from a *testimonia* source. For further analysis and parallels, see Albl, *Scripture Cannot Be Broken*, 155–57; Hvalvik, *Struggle*, 189–91; Carleton Paget, *Barnabas*, 154–56; Morgan-Wynne, *Holy Spirit*, 113–14.

32. Translation mine. Holmes reads *en pneumati* as "in our spirits," but I see no reason not to translate this in a manner consistent with its usage elsewhere in the epistle.

33. See further Hvalvik, *Struggle*, 190.

fact the Spirit, just as it was the Spirit who allowed people even before the incarnation of Christ to be Christians. To put this another way, the Spirit who allowed the Old Testament saints to look forward to Christ is the same Spirit who now through Scripture calls Christians to obedience and, in bringing the Spirit's future work into the present, is the same Spirit who empowers that present obedience through his eschatological pouring out on the people of God at baptism.

Thus, to bring this analysis of Barnabas to a close, it is ultimately the Holy Spirit that is the means by which the epistle can claim the Scriptures and the covenant of Judaism for Christianity. The reason for this is that the Spirit is the common link between the author's theological argument and the pneumatic experience that motivated and empowered his audience's distinctive early Christian identity. We have here evidence of a subtle strategy in which the author of Barnabas targets his audience's hearts as well as their minds, connecting their religious practice and experience with their theological understanding of how God operates across different dispensations of the divine economy. In this way, the Epistle of Barnabas fashions a Christian identity with respect to the Holy Spirit that is both unique and also deeply connected to other expressions of early Christianity. In so doing, the author of Barnabas has in effect Christianized the Spirit, claiming the Spirit even in Old Testament times as an agent of Christian faith. The next logical step in constructing a pneumatology on this basis would be taken by Justin Martyr, to whom we now turn.

Justin Martyr

Justin Martyr (ca. 100–165) was arguably the greatest of the early Christian apologists. A gentile convert to Christianity, Justin's quest for the true philosophy ultimately led him to embrace the Christian faith. At the height of his career, Justin moved to Rome, where he engaged in public disputation as well as the informal teaching of pupils in the model of a philosophical school; his extant literary corpus thus shows him to have been well-versed in Greco-Roman philosophy and rhetoric.[34] In the next chapter of this book we will explore Justin's most significant pneumatological innovation, which connected the Spirit's testifying function with a portrayal of the Spirit as a distinct person capable of engaging in dialogue with the Father and

34. For more on Justin's life, see Osborn, *Justin Martyr*, 6–10; Allert, *Revelation*, 28–31.

the Son. For now, however, we will examine another key aspect of Justin's pneumatology, which clearly builds upon the argument just observed in the Epistle of Barnabas.[35] In making the first explicit argument for the cessation of the Spirit from Judaism following the coming of Christ, Justin further contributed to the Christianization of the Spirit.

Like the author of Barnabas, Justin wrote in the context of the complex process of Christian self-definition with respect to Judaism. This is exemplified in his *Dialogue with Trypho*, a lengthy work written ca. 160 CE that purports to record an extended debate between Justin and a Jew named Trypho. In this text, we can see Justin at work fashioning a Christian identity set off as distinct from Judaism, which he believed to be a threat and competitor to his adopted faith.[36] The primary battleground, in Justin's mind, was over the correct interpretation of the Scriptures; while both Jews and Christians appealed to the same set of Scriptures, Justin argued for the superiority of Christian exegesis of the Old Testament on account of the Christians alone having accurately ascertained the true identity of Jesus as the Christ, the Logos of God.[37] It is in this broader context, then, that we can make sense of an important and original argument Justin makes concerning the Holy Spirit. First, however, we must identify how Justin grounds his understanding of Christian identity, in continuity with the authors of the New Testament and Barnabas, on the experience of the Holy Spirit.

The Experience of the Spirit

Justin's writings indicate that even as church structures became increasingly organized and hierarchical and even as Christian worship became increasingly fixed and formalized, the experience of the Spirit remained at the center of Christian identity.[38] As with Barnabas, Justin identifies Christians as those

---

35. This is not to insist that Justin had direct access to Barnabas, as it may be the case that Justin is drawing upon underlying *testimonia* sources shared by both; see further Skarsaune, *Proof from Prophecy*, 113.

36. On the purpose and audience of Justin's *Dialogue with Trypho*, see Skarsaune, *Proof from Prophecy*, 258–59.

37. See Boyarin, *Border Lines*, 37–73; Osborn, *Justin Martyr*, 87–95; Allert, *Revelation*, 221–53. By "Scriptures," I mean what Christians now call the Old Testament, as it is to these writings alone that Justin refers when he uses that term.

38. Skarsaune, *Shadow*, 340: "If we turn to the sources from the second- and third-century church, we meet believers who, at every step in their coming to faith and in their lives as Christians, experienced the Spirit as the mover and the life-giving force."

who have received the Spirit, an experience that would have taken place at baptism.[39] In fact, the centrality of the Spirit for Justin is such that his case for Jesus having been the Christ rests upon the Christian experience of the Spirit.[40] For Justin, the pouring out of the Spirit following the ascension of Christ into heaven fulfilled the prophecies of Ps 68:19 and Joel 2:28–29 and thereby further proved him to be the true Christ (*Dial.* 87.5–6). The Spirit, Justin claims, is worthy of worship alongside of the Father, the Son, and even, enigmatically, the army of good angels (*1 Apol.* 6.1–2).[41]

This is not, however, a purely abstract claim; Justin insists that the Spirit is alive and active in his community and appeals to that fact as evidence to justify his defense of Christianity. As Justin tells Trypho, his Jewish interlocutor, "Now, if you look around, you can see among us Christians both male and female endowed with charisms from the Spirit of God" (*Dial.* 88.1).[42] These gifts of the Holy Spirit, Justin argues, were given to believers according to their merits and included such things as wisdom, counsel, fortitude, healing, foreknowledge, teaching, and fear of the Lord (cf. *Dial.* 39.2, 87.5).[43] With this portion of his argument, Justin is following on the well-trodden path of his predecessors; it is only when he takes his argument a step further that he builds upon the already established connection between the Spirit and Christian identity.

It is worth pausing, however, to reflect on one other provocative feature of Justin's understanding of the Christian experience of the Spirit. In contrast to what is implied in texts such as the Pastoral Epistles, Justin clearly indicates that in his experience women shared in the possession of charismatic gifts (*Dial.* 88.1); if we read this in conjunction with his citation of Joel 2:28–29 (*Dial.* 87.6), it appears Justin is referring to female prophets, which is of course an interesting foreshadowing of the

---

39. *Dial.* 29.1; see further Morgan-Wynne, *Holy Spirit*, 165; Stanton, "Spirit in the Writings of Justin Martyr," 324–25.

40. Skarsaune, *Shadow*, 340, with reference to *Dial.* 87.4–6.

41. Stanton, "Spirit in the Writings of Justin Martyr," 329.

42. Translations from Justin's *Dialogue with Trypho* are taken from Falls, *Dialogue with Trypho*, unless otherwise noted.

43. This list of spiritual gifts was largely taken from Isa 11:1–3, which Justin and Trypho both took to be a prophecy of the Christ (*Dial.* 87.2). As Skarsaune (*Shadow*, 340 n. 2) notes, this passage was the foundation for the Jewish notion of the "sevenfold" Spirit given to the Messiah, an idea reflected in the New Testament at Rev 3:1. On the biblical roots of Justin's various lists of gifts, see Stanton, "Spirit in the Writings of Justin Martyr," 332.

Montanist movement that would begin a decade later.[44] Likewise, Justin elsewhere specifically mentions that "among us Christians the charisms of prophecy exist down to the present day" (*Dial.* 82.1), demonstrating that the Montanists were perhaps not as innovative in their appeal to continued prophecy as often thought.[45] While the connections between Justin and the Montanists are intriguing, what is most important for our purposes is the continued centrality of the experience of the Spirit, even in its more charismatic forms, well into the second century. This challenges any neat account of the "decline" of the experience of the Spirit or of the gifts of the Spirit; as Morgan-Wynne summarizes, "Justin Martyr, then, becomes evidence that in 'popular' Christianity of the mid-second century the experience of the Holy Spirit was part of the life and discipleship of Christians," with the Spirit unquestionably "an important ingredient in the life of the church."[46] We cannot know how representative Justin's claims were of all Christian communities in his time, but at minimum we are forced to consider reading our second-century sources in more of a charismatic light than we may have otherwise considered doing.

The Cessation of the Spirit from Judaism

We turn now to Justin's real innovation concerning the Spirit and Christian identity. Justin's approach to the Christianization of the Spirit is best glimpsed in his claim that the Spirit had been transferred from the Jews to the Christians. In *Dial.* 87, Justin argues that the present experience of the Spirit among Christians was the fulfillment of prophecy and the proof of Jesus' identity as the Christ. Justin observes that, before the coming of Christ, the central Old Testament figures all received some of the gifts of the Spirit; Solomon, for instance, was given "the spirit of wisdom" (*Dial.* 87.4). Christ, though, had all of the gifts of the Spirit bestowed upon him (*Dial.* 87.3).[47] The reason for this, Justin explains to Trypho, was that these gifts might cease among the Jews:

---

44. Stanton, "Spirit in the Writings of Justin Martyr," 333; Stanton (ibid.) also notes 2 *Apol.* 2.1–20 as evidence of the high status of women in the Roman church.

45. See Morgan-Wynne, *Holy Spirit*, 168.

46. Morgan-Wynne, *Holy Spirit*, 169–70.

47. For further discussion, see Skarsaune, *Proof from Prophecy*, 274–77; Morgan-Wynne, *Holy Spirit*, 167–69.

> The Spirit therefore rested, that is, ceased, when Christ came. For, after man's redemption was accomplished by him, these gifts were to cease among you, and, having come to an end in him, should again be given, as was foretold, by him, from the grace of the Spirit's powers, to all his believers in accordance with their merits.[48]

In other words, Justin tells Trypho concerning the Jews, Jesus intended that there would be "no more prophets among your people as of old, as is plainly evident to you, for after him there has not been a prophet among you" (*Dial.* 87.3). Here Justin makes a bold move, claiming that the (albeit partial and inferior) bestowal of the Spirit on the Jews ended with the incarnation of Christ, the Spirit having been transferred to the Christians. As Justin puts it succinctly elsewhere, "the gifts that previously resided among your people have now been transferred to us" (*Dial.* 82.1). It is not enough, for Justin, that the Spirit be Christianized and poured out upon the Christians; rather, the Spirit must now be denied to the Jews entirely. Not even the author of the Epistle of Barnabas ventured so bold a claim. Still, this argument appears to be part and parcel of Justin's broader claim that the church is the true Israel, with faith and the Spirit as the distinguishing features of Christianity over and against Judaism (cf. *Dial.* 135.3–6).[49]

Ironically, but continuing to demonstrate one of the major themes of this book, Justin developed this anti-Jewish view on the basis of his interpretation of the Old Testament. In the aforementioned passage from *Dial.* 87.5, Justin engages in something of a play on words, equating the verb meaning "to rest" with a related verb meaning "to cease" in his interpretation of Isa 11:2.[50] In so doing, Justin takes an Old Testament prophecy that suggested that the Spirit would rest in the sense of "rest upon" to instead mean that the Spirit would rest in the sense of "stop" or "cease." This had the advantage of avoiding the possible reading that there was a time when Christ lacked the Spirit (which was precisely Trypho's interpretation at *Dial.* 87.2) as well as, conveniently, denying the Spirit to the Jews in favor of the true Israel. Even on this latter point, Justin's notion of the church as the real Israel was rooted in his interpretation of Old Testament passages, in this case prophecies such as Isa 65:9–12 and Isa 2:5–6, which he quotes

---

48. *Dial.* 87.5.

49. Stanton, "Spirit in the Writings of Justin Martyr," 333–34.

50. Morgan-Wynne, *Holy Spirit*, 167 n. 94. The verbs here are *anapauomai* and *pauomai*.

in support of this very point at *Dial.* 135.3–6.[51] Indeed, on a broader scale, much of Justin's understanding of the Spirit was in fact grounded in the Old Testament and the traditions of Judaism. While both Justin and his Jewish interlocutors believed in the Spirit's inspiration of the Old Testament prophets, it was ultimately Justin's claim that their prophecies were fulfilled in Christ or in the present day that would prove to be "unacceptable and incomprehensible" to the Jews.[52]

For Justin, therefore, the Spirit belonged exclusively to the Christians. The Christian experience of the Spirit, a central mark of Christian identity from the beginning, was now used to draw a clear boundary line between two groups that had previously not been consistently seen as distinct or easily identifiable entities. It is not surprising, perhaps, that in his program of constructing a distinctively Christian identity, Justin would appeal to the Spirit; given the central role of the Spirit in the community, both at baptism and in the presence of various charismatic gifts, Justin's construction of a distinct group with the label of "Christian" on the basis of the possession of the Spirit would have resonated with his audience's lived experience.[53]

Conclusion

As we have seen in this chapter, the Epistle of Barnabas and Justin Martyr's writings bear witness to a lively debate concerning to whom the Spirit belonged, be it Jews or Christians. The Christian side of the argument, preserved in Barnabas and Justin, clearly demonstrates increased reflection on how the role of the Spirit changed as a result of the coming of Christ. The author of the Epistle of Barnabas, seeking to demonstrate the superiority of emerging Christianity over and against Judaism, claimed the Jewish Scriptures and covenant for Christianity. In order to make this claim, the author of the epistle argues that, by the Spirit, Old Testament patriarchs Abraham, Jacob, and Moses looked forward to Christ and were, therefore, themselves Christians. In fact, the Spirit himself looked forward to Christ and can be claimed for Christianity. The epistle connects this Spirit with the Spirit who is even now re-presenting Scripture to the community and is poured out upon believers at baptism, forging a link between the community's present

---

51. Stanton, "Spirit in the Writings of Justin Martyr," 333.

52. Stanton, "Spirit in the Writings of Justin Martyr," 334.

53. See also Hughes, "Spirit Speaks," 480–82, where I first began developing this line of argument.

experience of the Spirit with their understanding of the Spirit's work before the coming of Christ. Thus, the Spirit serves a distinctly Christian purpose in Barnabas, as the Spirit has in a sense always truly belonged to the Christians. For his part, Justin Martyr bears witness to the continuing importance of the experience of the Holy Spirit well into the second century, emphasizing the presence of charismatic gifts as a marker of Christian identity. Justin went beyond Barnabas in denying the Spirit to the Jews, instead insisting that the Spirit had been transferred to the Christians. Justin even used his interpretation of the Jews' own Scriptures to claim, on account of this transfer of the Spirit, that the Christians were the true Israel. By constructing his version of a distinct Christian identity on the basis of the very Spirit that was so central to his community, Justin further abetted the building of boundary lines between Christianity and Judaism.

Justin's claim that the Spirit had ceased from Judaism would have a long afterlife, recurring in the arguments of Irenaeus, Tertullian, and even the *Didascalia Apostolorum*.[54] The Spirit was, henceforth, truly and exclusively a possession of the Christians, or so at least Christian writers claimed. Still, exchanges between Jews and Christians continued. As scholars have demonstrated, interaction, tension, and hostility between Jews and Christians continued for centuries.[55] As we will see, however, the most significant battles over the Spirit will, from this point forward, be fought among different groups laying claim to the name "Christian." In assessing the Christianizing of the Spirit, as carried out by the author of Barnabas and Justin, we must be attentive to the extent to which these Christian writers took over, rather than rejected, the Old Testament as a source for theologizing about the Spirit. It was ultimately this position, rather than that of Marcion, which would have rejected the Old Testament altogether, that would of course set the stage for all further reflection on the Spirit. The price for this move of co-opting the Scriptures, covenant, and indeed even the Spirit of Judaism was, however, high, with the unfortunate seeds of anti-Semitism being planted in the process.

Moving our eyes to the next major tile in the mosaic, we are admittedly a bit surprised. Whereas previously we could have pictured this mosaic adorning a Jewish synagogue, the presence of this tile representing the Christianization of the Spirit means that from this point forward

---

54. Morgan-Wynne, *Holy Spirit*, 317–23, with reference to Irenaeus, *Haer.* 3.17.3–4; Tertullian, *Adv. Jud.* 8.13, 13.15, 13.25; *Adv. Marc.* 3.23, 5.8; *Did. Ap.* 23.5.7.

55. See especially Wilken, *Judaism and the Early Christian Mind*.

we can only envision this particular mosaic in the context of a Christian church. The original contributors to the mosaic may not have anticipated the later addition of this tile, but if we gaze at it long enough we can begin to grasp some of the logic by which its creators believed it to line up with the earlier tiles. Like the tiles placed before it, this tile was crafted from the material of biblical exegesis and was placed with the adhesive of pneumatic experience. Most of all, though, we are struck by how the placement of this tile next to the tile representing the Spirit's provision of divine testimony, a tile still giving off that faint glow suggesting personhood, generates one of the most creative and significant portions of the entire mosaic, as we will see in the next chapter of this book.

CHAPTER 4

The Spirit and Person Language

As Christianity expanded in the second and third centuries, it was confronted by challenges, not just from Jews, but also from within, as different groups claiming the label "Christian" fought over the future of the faith. One of the primary battlegrounds on which the war for Christian identity was contested was over the correct interpretation of the Scriptures—that is, the Old Testament. In their analysis of this issue, scholars have recently been increasingly attentive to the debt that early Christian exegetes owed to the principles of interpretation taken from the world of classical rhetoric. Specifically, as the work of Frances Young has demonstrated, the Scriptures became viewed as a new set of literature that could be studied using the exegetical practices that were taught in Greco-Roman schools. As there began to emerge distinctively Christian schools based on the study of the Scriptures, these schools very logically adopted the habits and assumptions of the broader culture regarding how to understand, interpret, and apply written texts.[1] Thanks to the preservation of ancient rhetorical textbooks, we have a glimpse into how early Christian exegetes would have approached their work.[2]

In this chapter, we will examine how one of the elements in this interpretive process, which focused on identifying the speakers or the audience of certain dialogical passages, was applied to the reading of Scripture in such a way as to endow upon the Spirit a greater degree of personhood. In order to fully tell the story of this particular pneumatological trajectory, we will have to survey three important early Christian exegetes: Justin Martyr, Irenaeus of Lyons, and Tertullian of Carthage. In sum, whereas the previous chapter

---

1. Young, *Biblical Exegesis*, 76.
2. See further Young, *Biblical Exegesis*, 77–81.

of this book considered how the relationship between emergent Christianity and Judaism contributed to pneumatological innovation, this chapter allows us to explore the influence of Greco-Roman rhetoric on the process by which the Spirit became God. First, though, we will need to consider in more detail the specific element of the classical interpretive process known in the scholarly literature today as prosopological exegesis.

Prosopological Exegesis

In their reading of the Hebrew Scriptures, early Christian exegetes stumbled across many puzzles. One such interpretive dilemma involved scenes of dialogue in which the speaker or audience was perceived to be unclear. The Psalter and the Prophets, for example, feature many dialogical passages with frequent, abrupt shifts in speaking characters that pose substantial interpretive challenges. In response to these texts in which the speakers or addressees were unclear or ambiguous, early Christian writers sought to explain how, in light of the emerging Christian understanding of unity and diversity in the Godhead, these riddles could be solved through the identification of multiple divine speakers. Modern scholars use the term "prosopological exegesis" to describe this early Christian practice of identifying the various "characters" or "persons" (Greek *prosōpa*; Latin *personae*) participating in dialogical passages in the Old Testament.[3]

We see this process at work in the New Testament itself. For instance, in Mark 12:35–37 and parallels, Jesus debates the scribes on the right interpretation of the characters referred to in a famous scene of Old Testament dialogue. Jesus quotes the words of David in Ps 110:1: "The Lord said to my Lord, 'Sit at my right hand, until I put your enemies under your feet'" (Mark 12:36). Responding to the scribal claim that the Messiah is the son of David, Jesus proceeds to argue that "David himself calls him Lord; so how can he be his son?" (Mark 12:37). In other words, the logic appears to be, the audience for the dialogue spoken in Ps 110:1, referred to by David as "my Lord," must be someone greater than simply David's son; indeed, the rest of

---

3. A more technical definition of prosopological exegesis is provided by Bates, *Hermeneutics*, 218: "Prosopological exegesis is a reading technique whereby an interpreter seeks to overcome a real or perceived ambiguity regarding the identity of the speakers or addressees (or both) in the divinely inspired source text by assigning nontrivial prosopa (i.e., nontrivial vis-à-vis the 'plain sense' of the text) to the speakers or addressees (or both) in order to make sense of the text." For an overview of the history of scholarship on prosopological exegesis, see Bates, *Hermeneutics*, 183–87.

the psalm, activated by reference to this opening verse, seems to portray this figure as preexistent and divinely begotten.[4] In his person-centered reading of this Old Testament dialogue, Jesus has used the undergirding logic of the text to subversively redefine the notion of Davidic messiahship;[5] as Richard Hays concludes concerning this passage, "Jesus is not just the anointed king awaited by Israel; he enjoys a still higher dignity."[6] Thus, we can speak of prosopological exegesis as being an important reading strategy from the very beginning of the Christian movement.[7]

Likewise, Paul frequently employed prosopological exegesis in his interpretation of the Old Testament. To take just one example, in Rom 15:3, Paul attributes the words of David in Ps 69:9 ("the insults of those who insult you have fallen on me") to Christ, identifying Christ as their ultimate speaker and thereby presenting a theodramatic scene in which the enthroned Christ recounts to God the Father his experience on the cross.[8] The upshot of all of this is that the prosopological exegesis employed by the church fathers to develop the personhood of the Holy Spirit is very much a New Testament phenomenon. There is, therefore, a hermeneutical continuity between the New Testament writers and the Christian exegetes of the first centuries.

Three features of prosopological exegesis are worth further exploration at this stage. First, in undertaking such a person-centered reading strategy, these early Christian exegetes were simply adopting what was considered good interpretive practice in the Greco-Roman schools of the time. According to ancient rhetorical handbooks, one of the steps in analyzing a text was to identify the different persons or characters who were speaking or being addressed. The Greek term for such a person, *prosōpon*, had its origins in the classical theater, where it referred to a mask that an actor would take on or off in order to distinguish between multiple characters.[9] Thus, when

---

4. For further analysis of this passage through the insights of prosopological exegesis, see Bates, *Birth*, 44–56. On the assumed invitation to consider the psalm as a whole, see Dodd, *According to the Scriptures*, 126; Hays, *Echoes of Scripture in the Letters of Paul*, 25–33.

5. Cf. Hays, *Echoes of Scripture in the Gospels*, 53–57.

6. Hays, *Echoes of Scripture in the Gospels*, 57.

7. Bates (*Birth*, 203) attributes this interpretation to the historical Jesus himself; in any case, we are here dealing with tradition from the first decades of the Christian movement.

8. See further Bates, *Hermeneutics*, 240–55.

9. On what is called *prosopopoeia* in the ancient rhetorical setting, see Bates,

early Christian writers used prosopological exegesis to help make sense of an Old Testament dialogue, they were appealing to a reading strategy that would have been widely understood and accepted in the ancient world. The debates we will examine in this chapter, therefore, were over the results of this method, not the method itself.

Second, the theatrical and literary backgrounds of prosopological exegesis should caution us against drawing hasty conclusions regarding the significance of the person-language used in early Christian applications of this method. Matthew Bates uses the term "theodrama" in order to describe "the dramatic world invoked by an ancient reader of Scripture as that reader construed a prophet to be speaking from or observing the person (*prosōpon*) of a divine or human character."[10] This language of "theodrama" reminds us that the person-language used in prosopological exegesis was, at least initially, meant to be understood metaphorically, with little concern for fleshing out a further picture of what such personhood might entail on the ontological level. As Bates prudently instructs us, "when we speak of divine persons as revealed through scriptural interpretation, the *quality* of personhood is necessarily metaphorically determined."[11] As we will see, though, this understanding of personhood will in fact change in highly significant ways over time.

Third, while recent scholarship has analyzed in great detail how early Christian exegetes employed prosopological exegesis in identifying theodramatic conversations between the Father and the Son in the pages of the Old Testament, precious little attention has been devoted to exploring those instances in which the Holy Spirit was identified as a participant in one of these divine dialogues.[12] Undoubtedly a major reason for this oversight is the fact that in the vast majority of instances in which the Spirit is identified as the "speaker" of an Old Testament text, the author simply means that the Spirit was the inspiring force behind the writing of Scripture, both in a general sense and more specifically as the one who inspired the prophets to slip into the role of an actor in the divine theodrama. That being said, there are a handful of important instances in which the Spirit

---

Hermeneutics, 194–99; on ancient drama as a background for prosopological exegesis, see Bates, *Hermeneutics*, 192–94.

10. Bates, *Birth*, 5 n. 8.

11. Bates, *Birth*, 38 (italics original).

12. For an overview of the limited scholarship on the relationship between the Spirit and prosopological exegesis, see Hughes, *Trinitarian Testimony*, 12–21.

is portrayed as participating in divine dialogues as his own person. To differentiate between these two senses in which the Spirit relates to the words of Scripture, Bates has introduced the terms "inspiring secondary agent" and "primary speaking agent" to describe each of these respective phenomena.[13] While I have elsewhere set out criteria by which to distinguish between these two senses across all early Christian literature,[14] in this chapter we will exclusively focus on passages in which the Spirit is portrayed as a primary speaking agent, for it is upon these texts that early Christian conceptions of the Spirit's distinct personhood will be built. We will now trace the link between prosopological exegesis and the personhood of the Spirit in the three aforementioned pre-Nicene writers (Justin, Irenaeus, and Tertullian), considering especially the ways in which the nature of this personhood evolved from writer to writer.

Justin Martyr

Justin Martyr (ca. 100–165), to whom we were introduced in the previous chapter of this book, was by training a philosopher, and his extant writings give a wealth of evidence to demonstrate his understanding of ancient literary conventions. Indeed, as we will see shortly, Justin was not only himself conversant in the principles of ancient exegesis, but he also assumed his readers were familiar with such strategies as applied to pagan literature. Justin thus stands out as one of the first instances in which a Christian teacher of philosophy "lays claim to an ancient literary heritage," thereby more formally bringing to bear all the principles of interpretation set out by classical rhetoric.[15] We see this clearly, for instance, in Justin's explicit and systematic use of prosopological exegesis, to which we now turn.

Justin and Prosopological Exegesis

Justin is the first extant Christian writer to explicitly and systematically make use of the person-centered reading strategy that scholars call prosopological exegesis. In his *1 Apology* (ca. 155), Justin provides an overview of his prosopological approach to interpreting the Old Testament:

13. Bates, *Birth*, 164 n. 18.
14. Hughes, "Spirit and the Scriptures," 38–41.
15. Young, *Biblical Exegesis*, 67.

> But when you hear the sayings of the prophets spoken as from the person of someone, do not suppose they are spoken from the inspired persons themselves, but from the divine Word who moves them. For sometimes He speaks as one announcing beforehand things that are about to happen, but sometimes He speaks as from the person of God, the Father and Master of all, and still other times as from the person of Christ, and at still other times from the person of the people answering the Lord or His Father, just as you can see even in your own writers, one man being the composer of the whole, but introducing the persons who converse.[16]

Thus, for Justin, the "divine Word" in its inspiration of Scripture can take on and off different masks, speaking in turn from each of these different "persons" or "characters" (*prosōpa*). As the conclusion of this quotation confirms, Justin's appeal to this person-centered reading strategy would have been familiar to his audience. Justin goes on to insist that his careful use of this reading strategy justifies the superiority of his interpretation of Scripture over that of the Jews, whom he claimed were neglecting to follow this basic step in analyzing a text (*1 Apol.* 36.3). In the following section of his apology, Justin proceeds to give examples of quotations that he believes should be understood as having been spoken in the person of the Father (*1 Apol.* 37), the person of the Son (*1 Apol.* 38), and the prophetic Spirit (*1 Apol.* 39–45).[17]

It is the introduction of the Spirit in this context that actually creates some significant interpretive challenges. On the one hand, Justin's aforementioned overview of his use of prosopological exegesis identifies the "divine Word," or Logos, as the one speaking in the form of these different characters. On the other hand, however, Justin elsewhere consistently designates the Holy Spirit as the one doing this work.[18] This tension is best resolved by recognizing that Justin largely operated under a paradigm of angelomorphic pneumatology that allowed for overlap between the functions and even the identity of the Word and the Spirit. Therefore, this general work of inspiring Scripture is perhaps best understood as an

16. *1 Apol.* 36.1–2; translations from *1 Apology* are taken from Barnard, *First and Second Apologies*. On this passage, see further Bates, *Hermeneutics*, 199–204; Hughes, *Trinitarian Testimony*, 36–38.

17. Interestingly, in *1 Apol.* 39–45, the Spirit simply inspires the words of the prophets; the notion of dialogue between divine persons, as in *1 Apol.* 37–38, has fallen out of view. See further Hughes, *Trinitarian Testimony*, 54–58.

18. See, e.g., *1 Apol.* 38.1, 44.1, 47.1, 53.6, 61.13; *Dial.* 7.1.

action of the Spirit as it participates in the Word.[19] Even despite Justin's clear reliance on a form of Spirit Christology, Justin at times nevertheless begins to move beyond an essentially binitarian understanding of God to one that looks increasingly trinitarian.[20] Indeed, one of the ways in which a more trinitarian understanding emerges in Justin's writing is through his use of prosopological exegesis insofar as the Spirit is not only the power by which the prophets and other divine persons speak but also, in a few tantalizing instances, presented as participating in divine conversations *as his own person* (*prosōpon*).

Justin's Portrayal of the Spirit as a *Prosōpon*

One of the important themes in Justin's *Dialogue with Trypho* (ca. 160) concerns the claim that Christians believe in a "second God," that is, Christ, in addition to the Creator. In one exchange on this subject, Trypho, Justin's Jewish interlocutor, challenges Justin to prove from Scripture that "the prophetic Spirit ever admits the existence of another God, besides the Creator of all things" (*Dial.* 55.1). Justin's response is to cite some famous "two powers" texts, so-called because they were used by early Christians to argue for the presence of the Word alongside of the Father. In a key passage, Justin uses prosopological exegesis to interpret some of these texts:

> "Not only because of that quotation [that is, Gen 19:23–25, which had been quoted above]," I said, "must we certainly admit that, besides the Creator of the universe, another was called Lord by the Holy Spirit. For this was attested to not only by Moses, but also by David, when he said, *The Lord said to my Lord: Sit at my right hand, until I make your enemies your footstool* [Ps 110:1]. And in other words, *Your throne, O God, is forever and ever; the scepter of your kingdom is a scepter of uprightness. You have loved justice, and hated iniquity; therefore God, your God, has anointed you with the oil of gladness above your fellow kings* [Ps 45:6–7]. Tell me if it is your opinion that the Holy Spirit calls another *God* and *Lord*, besides the Father of all things and his Christ."[21]

19. Cf. Bates, *Hermeneutics*, 200.

20. On this tension in Justin with reference to his pneumatology, see Briggman, "Justin's Approach," 107–37.

21. *Dial.* 56.14; translations of Justin's *Dialogue* are from Falls, *Dialogue with Trypho*, unless otherwise noted. On this passage, see further Hughes, *Trinitarian Testimony*, 33–34, 38–46.

Leaving aside the reference to Gen 19:23–25,[22] we can focus on Justin's prosopological reading of the dialogical passages quoted from Ps 110:1 and Ps 45:6–7. As we saw at the beginning of this chapter, Mark 12:35–37 and its parallels present a prosopological reading of Ps 110:1 in which David, glimpsing this scene in the divine theodrama, observes "the Lord" (that is, the Father) speaking to "my Lord" (that is, the Son). While acknowledging that David is the human author who records the words of Ps 110:1, Justin proceeds a step forward by introducing the Spirit into this theodramatic setting. As the framing words around the biblical citations indicate, there is a third person, identified by Justin as the Spirit, who is observing and reporting this theodramatic speech and therefore ascribing to both the Father and the Son the title "Lord." David is thus recording a theodramatic moment in which the Spirit is reporting the words of the Father to the Son.[23]

Likewise, in his interpretation of Ps 45:6–7 Justin finds a theodramatic role for the Spirit. In this case, the Spirit is speaking directly to the Son, telling Christ of his eternal reign and recalling the Father's anointing of the Son. Here there is no question that the Spirit is portrayed as a theodramatic person in his own right, engaging in dialogue with the Son concerning the Father. Indeed, the verbs for "to call 'Lord'" (kyriologeō) and "to call 'God'" (theologeō) seem to demand a personal subject, and thus this appears to be an example of what Bates terms the Spirit speaking as a "primary speaking agent" insofar as the Spirit is presented as participating in the divine theodrama as his own person rather than in the guise of another.[24]

This is a remarkable moment in the history of the development of the doctrine of the Holy Spirit. What Justin is here suggesting is nothing less than that the Scriptures bear witness to the internal conversations of the Godhead. The Spirit, himself the inspirer of the Scriptures, is here portrayed as a participant in conversations whereby the divine persons testify to one another. It is as if the curtains of heaven are ripped back and we are privileged to catch a glimpse of theology in the making, overhearing God's own thoughts about himself. To return to our discussion in chapter 2 of this book, here we have a tangible picture of what it means that the Spirit "searches everything,

---

22. See my discussion in Hughes, *Trinitarian Testimony*, 41–42.

23. On Justin's text of Ps 110:1, see Skarsaune, *Proof from Prophecy*, 86–88; on Ps 110:1 as a *testimonium* in early Christianity more broadly, see Albl, *Scripture Cannot Be Broken*, 216–36; Hay, *Glory at the Right Hand*.

24. On Justin's text of Ps 45:6–7, see Skarsaune, *Proof from Prophecy*, 126; on Ps 45:6–7 as a *testimonium* in early Christianity more broadly, see Albl, *Scripture Cannot Be Broken*, 205–6.

even the depths of God" (1 Cor 2:10). The implication of this scene, even if Justin does not tease this out in full, is that the Spirit is a distinct and coequal participant in this internal divine discourse.

One possible objection to this reading is that the language of "person" (*prosōpon*) is not explicitly used in this passage, and so perhaps we should understand the Spirit's function here as merely that of an "inspiring secondary agent." Is it really the case, the objection runs, that Justin believed the Spirit could speak theodramatically as his own person? After all, Justin's overview of prosopological exegesis in *1 Apol.* 36 does not mention the "person" of the Spirit. This objection, however, is not sustainable. Besides the evidence presented above, we can turn to another passage in the *Dialogue* for final confirmation that Justin did indeed believe that the Spirit could speak from his own person. In response to Trypho's demand for scriptural proof that Jesus is indeed the promised and now glorified Messiah (*Dial.* 36.1), Justin responds with a christological interpretation of Ps 24 (*Dial.* 36.5). At the end of his analysis of this psalm, Justin acknowledges a puzzle over the identity of the speaker who responds to a question posed by the angels who are observing the ascension of Christ:

> For when the heavenly rulers saw that his appearance was unsightly, dishonored, and inglorious, not recognizing him, they inquired, *Who is this King of Glory?* And the Holy Spirit, either from the person of the Father or from his own person answered, *The Lord of Hosts. He is the King of Glory* [Ps 24:10].[25]

Per the conventions of ancient rhetoric, Justin is trying to identify the various persons in a dialogical passage featuring abrupt shifts in speaking characters. In his attempt to provide a prosopological interpretation of the text, Justin admits he cannot decide whether Ps 24:10b is spoken by the Spirit "from the person of the Father" (thus as an inspiring secondary agent; cf. *1 Apol.* 36.1–2) or "from his own person" (thus as a primary speaking agent; cf. *Dial.* 56.14–15). While he does not come to a firm conclusion, this does prove that Justin did indeed believe that the Spirit could possibly speak as his own person (*prosōpon*).[26] The juxtaposition of these two interpretive

---

25. *Dial.* 36.6 (translation mine). On this passage, see further Hughes, *Trinitarian Testimony*, 59–61.

26. Justin's difficulty seems to result from two conflicting preferences: one that the Spirit is the person who testifies to the deity and the lordship of Christ, and one that the Father is the person who speaks concerning the Son outside of "two powers" texts such as those found in *Dial.* 56.14–15. See further Hughes, *Trinitarian Testimony*, 61.

options clearly shows that the Spirit does not simply inspire the prophets or take on the role of other characters (though this is the Spirit's usual role in relation to the words of Scripture), but can at times fully participate in these divine dialogues as a person in his own right.

Interestingly, this passage appears to indicate a similar conception of the Spirit's work in the divine theodrama as what we observed in the case of *Dial.* 56.14–15. Though Justin does not use the verbs for "to call 'Lord'" (*kyriologeō*) and "to call 'God'" (*theologeō*) in his interpretation of this passage, the Spirit's words in Ps 24:10 do include calling Christ "Lord," just as the Spirit was portrayed as calling Christ "Lord" in the words of Ps 110:1 and calling Christ "God" in the words of Ps 45:6–7. That this could merely be a coincidence is unlikely; rather, these data points suggest a pattern that, on further examination of all instances of Justin's use of prosopological exegesis, is confirmed: only the Spirit is portrayed as providing testimony to the divinity and lordship of other divine persons (that is, the Father and the Son).[27] To return to our discussion in chapter 2 of this book, this is an example of an appeal to the proof of divine testimony, with the Spirit providing this testimony through the words of Scripture. What is particularly interesting, though, as opposed to the conventions of Greco-Roman rhetoric, is that the Spirit's divine testimony is employed not merely to signal divine approval of a human being but rather to endow upon other divine persons the titles of "Lord" and, even, "God." This unique quality of the Spirit, in which the Spirit testifies as a divine person to the lordship or divinity of another divine person, I have elsewhere termed *intra-divine testimony* or, more specifically when all three persons of the Trinity are in view (as in Ps 110:1 and Ps 45:6–7), *trinitarian testimony*.[28] That this would be a function assigned exclusively to the Spirit seems to me to be a logical outgrowth of the Johannine portrayal of the Spirit as providing true testimony concerning the person and work of Christ (cf. John 15:26). Moreover, that the Spirit would thus testify through the words of Scripture seems to logically follow from the assumptions made about the Old Testament as belonging to the Christians and inspired by the Christianized Spirit, points that were discussed in chapter 3 above. In sum, then, Justin has made a significant innovation with respect to the Spirit, albeit one that

27. For a full analysis of all relevant data, see Hughes, *Trinitarian Testimony*, 46–63. This confirms the observation of Briggman, "Justin's Approach," 113: "Justin also distinguishes the activity of the Spirit by attributing to it a special role in testifying to the deity and sovereignty of the Father and Son."

28. See further Hughes, *Trinitarian Testimony*, 44–45.

is very much in continuity with these preceding ideas, when he portrays the Spirit as a person participating in a divine theodrama that clearly reflects a Christian understanding of God.

What, though, did it mean for Justin that the Spirit was a "person"? Again, the context of prosopological exegesis and the concept of the divine theodrama are helpful in cautioning us against reading too much into what Justin is suggesting. As Bates has reminded us, early Christian exegetes employing prosopological exegesis, reflecting the reading strategy's background in drama, used person-language in a way that must be understood as largely metaphorical.[29] Still, there is a sense in which the Spirit, having been portrayed as a distinct actor in the divine theodrama, can be conceived of as having a greater degree of personhood than he would otherwise have if he were merely responsible for the inspiration of Scripture.[30] That this was the case is clear from the way subsequent exegetes who used prosopological exegesis from the person of the Spirit would continue a trajectory that would further shape and give definition to the Spirit as a distinct divine person. To continue this story, therefore, we turn to the witness of Irenaeus.

Irenaeus

Irenaeus of Lyons (ca. 135–200), famous for his defense (or, according to some, construction) of Christian orthodoxy, was born in Asia Minor before he moved west, presumably via Rome, to settle in modern-day France, where he served as a presbyter and then as bishop.[31] Irenaeus is best known for his massive treatise *Against Heresies*, which sought to refute the teachings of a broad and diverse movement known as Gnosticism, which was characterized by its teaching concerning a complicated cosmology populated by many emanations of the deity called Aeons.[32] Irenaeus serves as a further witness to the importance of the experience of the Holy Spirit for

29. See again Bates, *Birth*, 38.

30. The precise nature of Justin's ontology of personhood is ultimately unclear with respect to the Spirit. It is certainly possible that Justin's use of prosopological exegesis pushed him in the direction of the Spirit truly, in the ontological sense, being a distinct divine person, but in any event the notion is not explicit as it will be for Tertullian.

31. For recent overviews of Irenaeus' life, see Osborn, *Irenaeus*, 1–7; Minns, *Irenaeus*, 1–13; Lashier, *Irenaeus on the Trinity*, 18–41.

32. The term "Gnosticism" is problematic but still widely used in the literature; for discussion see further King, *What is Gnosticism?*; Lewis, *Introduction to "Gnosticism"*; Williams, *Rethinking "Gnosticism."*

early Christianity. Though we will explore this more in the next chapter of this book, for now we may simply note, following Morgan-Wynne, that for Irenaeus "the heart of Christianity is the experience of the Spirit," and indeed "the hallmark of the church and its members is the possession of the Spirit."[33] Recent scholarship has done much to demonstrate the significance of Irenaeus' pneumatology, focusing on how his synthesis of Jewish and Christian traditions concerning the Spirit resulted in a mature, elevated portrait of the person and work of the Spirit that more clearly distinguished the Spirit from the Son than had his predecessors such as Justin.[34] For our purposes, however, we will want to focus on one aspect of Irenaeus' pneumatology that has remained overlooked: his use of prosopological exegesis with respect to the person of the Spirit. It is here, as we will see, that Irenaeus made his greatest contribution to the emerging identity of the Spirit as a distinct divine person.

Irenaeus and Prosopological Exegesis

Like Justin, whose writings he appears to have been familiar with, Irenaeus made significant use of prosopological exegesis.[35] Given, though, that his gnostic opponents also utilized this person-centered reading strategy, Irenaeus was careful to set out clear principles by which he could argue for the superiority of his reading.[36] The different polemical context in which Irenaeus was writing is helpful for identifying both continuities and discontinuities with the use of prosopological exegesis by his predecessor Justin. For instance, following Justin, Irenaeus sets forth in his *Demonstration of the Apostolic Preaching* (ca. 190) an overview of his understanding of what we call prosopological exegesis (*Epid.* 49–50). As part of validating his claim that the Scriptures (in this case, the Old Testament) prove the eternal existence of Christ, Irenaeus aims to show that David spoke of both the Father and the Son. As evidence, Irenaeus appeals to Ps

33. Morgan-Wynne, *Holy Spirit*, 198, with reference to *Haer.* 4.33.15 and 4.36.22. For full survey, see Morgan-Wynne, *Holy Spirit*, 195–218.

34. See further Barnes, "Beginning and End," 170–80; Briggman, *Irenaeus*, 32–215; Lashier, *Irenaeus on the Trinity*, 149–88.

35. On Irenaeus' reliance on Justin, see Lashier, *Irenaeus on the Trinity*, 22–26. Slusser, "Irenaeus," 515–20, even goes so far as to suggest that Irenaeus was one of Justin's students in Rome.

36. On Irenaeus' use of prosopological exegesis, see Presley, "Exegetical Roots," 166–71; Bates, *Birth*, 183–88; cf. *Haer.* 1.8.1, 1.10.1.

2:7–8, noting that Christ, and not David (as the psalm's assumed author), received the things that were promised by God in this psalm. This brings Irenaeus to make the following conclusion:

> Since David says, *the Lord says to me* [Ps 2:7], it is necessary to affirm that it is not David nor any other one of the prophets, who speaks from himself—for it is not man who utters prophecies—but that the Spirit of God, conforming Himself to the person concerned, spoke in the prophets, producing words sometimes from Christ and at other times from the Father.[37]

As this passage demonstrates, Irenaeus, following Justin, believes that the right interpretation of Old Testament dialogical passages necessitates identifying the various "persons" (likely *prosōpa* in Irenaeus' Greek, which is no longer extant) who are conversing in the divine theodrama. Notably, Irenaeus has assigned the task of speaking as these different persons to the Holy Spirit. This is a helpful clarification of what seemed more muddled in Justin, who did little to distinguish between the work of the Logos and the Spirit in this capacity, and reflects Irenaeus' clearer conception of God as Trinity.[38] As with Justin, though, Irenaeus' introduction to prosopological exegesis only describes the Spirit's potential to function as an inspiring secondary agent. To find evidence of the Spirit functioning as a *primary* speaking agent, then, we will have to turn to another passage in Irenaeus' writings.

Irenaeus' Portrayal of the Spirit as a *Prosōpon*

In book 3 of his *Against Heresies* (ca. 185), Irenaeus is arguing, against the gnostics, that the Scriptures show that the Father and the Son are one and the same God. The Valentinian gnostics with whom Irenaeus is here in dialogue held that the creator god was an ignorant, spiritually inferior being far removed from the true Father God. For Irenaeus, however, there is only one true God, in whom the Son is included alongside of the Father. As evidence of this claim, Irenaeus, starting in *Haer.* 3.6.1, seeks to demonstrate from the Scriptures how the titles "God" and "Lord" are reserved for only the Father and the Son. To this end, Irenaeus makes the following comment concerning the names ascribed to the Son in the Scriptures:

---

37. *Epid.* 49; translations of the *Demonstration* are taken from Behr, *On the Apostolic Preaching*. On this passage, see further Hughes, *Trinitarian Testimony*, 106–10.

38. On Irenaeus' trinitarian theology, see further Lashier, *Irenaeus on the Trinity*.

Therefore, neither the Lord, nor the Holy Spirit, nor the apostles would precisely and absolutely ever have named "God" [*etheologēsan*] one who is not God, unless He truly was God. Nor would they, in their own name [*prosōpou*], have called anyone Lord [*ekyriolektēsan*] except God the Father who has dominion over all things, and His Son who received from His Father power over all creation, as is expressed in this passage: *The Lord said to my Lord, sit at my right hand, until I make your enemies your footstool* [Ps 110:1]. This shows the Father speaking to the Son, who gave to Him the inheritance of the Gentiles and subjected to Him all enemies. Since, therefore, the Father is truly Lord, and the Son truly Lord, the Holy Spirit deservedly designated them by the title "Lord."[39]

In this passage, Irenaeus' concern to discern the identities of the speaker and addressee in a dialogical passage of Scripture suggests a further instance of prosopological exegesis, which is confirmed by the appeal to how different characters speak "in their own name," which is better translated "from their own persons" in order to better capture the use of the term *prosōpou*. Notably, the Spirit is included alongside of the Lord and the apostles as capable of speaking from his own *prosōpon*, clarifying that he can function not merely as an inspiring secondary agent but indeed, as here, as a primary speaking agent in his own right.

A comparison with Justin is instructive: like his predecessor, Irenaeus identifies the Spirit as the speaker of Ps 110:1 for the purpose of testifying to the divinity and lordship of the Father and the Son (note again the appearance of forms of the verbs *kyriologeō* and *theologeō*). However, Irenaeus has dropped any references to David as the human speaker of Ps 110:1, further underscoring the notion that the Spirit is the ultimate theodramatic speaker of these words. Perhaps most interesting is how Irenaeus uses the same verse and the same interpretive method to arrive at a very different point: whereas Justin was concerned to expand the referent of the term "God" to be inclusive of multiple divine persons, Irenaeus, in the context of his conflict with Gnosticism, instead sought to emphasize the unity of God.[40] In both cases, though, we have a clear example of what I have above termed the trinitarian testimony of the Spirit. As with Justin,

---

39. *Haer.* 3.6.1; translations of *Against Heresies* are taken from Steenberg, *Against the Heresies*. On this passage, see further Hughes, *Trinitarian Testimony*, 110–14.

40. On Irenaeus' context, and in particular the Valentinian view of the cosmos and the various Aeons, see Thomassen, *Spiritual Seed*, 193–247.

Irenaeus appears to have judged the provision of trinitarian testimony to be a work exclusively reserved for the Spirit.[41]

Indeed, lest we have any doubts that Irenaeus is intentionally following the line of argument set down by Justin (albeit for his own purposes), we find that Irenaeus continues in this passage by quoting Gen 19:24 and Ps 45:6–7, the other "two powers" texts that Justin had also included alongside of Ps 110:1 in *Dial.* 56.14. Irenaeus argues that Ps 45:6–7 is evidence that "the Spirit designates both of them by the title 'God': the Son who is anointed and the Father who anoints" (*Haer.* 3.6.1). Therefore, on account of the specific lexical, thematic, and scriptural parallels between *Dial.* 56.14 and *Haer.* 3.6.1, we can establish an essential continuity between Justin and Irenaeus as it concerns their understanding of the Spirit theodramatically testifying to the divinity and lordship of the Father and the Son.

This basic continuity helps us keep in mind that Irenaeus, like Justin, seems to still have conceived of the Spirit's personhood in theodramatic, rather than ontological, terms.[42] But what Irenaeus has accomplished is to clarify, within the divine theodrama, that the Spirit is *a distinct divine person*. On account of his more clearly trinitarian-shaped theology, Irenaeus has carved out a unique identity and role for the Spirit apart from the Son. This is seen not only in Irenaeus' decision to attribute all prosopological exegesis to the inspiring work of the Spirit but also in his removal of references to the human prophet from descriptions of the Spirit's speech in his capacity as a primary speaking agent. For the next step in constructing the personhood of the Spirit through the use of prosopological exegesis, however, we turn to a successor of Irenaeus, Tertullian of Carthage.

Tertullian

Tertullian of Carthage (ca. 160–215), the fiery North African known both for his defense of orthodoxy and his embrace of the charismatic and rigorous "heresy" known as the New Prophecy (often anachronistically given the label "Montanism"), gives us a glimpse into the early world of North

---

41. See further Hughes, *Trinitarian Testimony*, 117–33.

42. As with Justin, it is possible that Irenaeus in fact conceived of the personhood of the Spirit in ontological terms and that this notion is embedded in his utilization of prosopological exegesis, but the absence of an explicit claim to this effect renders a more modest conclusion preferable for our analysis.

African Christianity as it developed distinctive beliefs and rituals.[43] Among Tertullian's thirty-one extant treatises, we find writings ranging from apologies directed to non-Christians, doctrinal writings targeted at heretics, and practical texts aimed at other Christians; across all genres, his rhetoric is sharply, at times even harshly, polemical.[44] Like Irenaeus, Tertullian testifies to the continued importance of early Christian experience of the Holy Spirit. Though we will save a more complete analysis for the next chapter of this book, there can be no question of Tertullian's belief in the continued activity of the Holy Spirit, particularly as it relates to prophecy and guiding Christians into a lifestyle of firm discipline.[45] Tertullian's significance for the development of early Christian pneumatology is well-established in the literature,[46] but here we will focus specifically on his contribution as it results from his use of prosopological exegesis.

Tertullian and Prosopological Exegesis

Like his predecessors Justin and Irenaeus, Tertullian frequently appealed to prosopological exegesis in his interpretation of the Old Testament. Given that scholars believe Tertullian had access to the writings of both Justin and Irenaeus, we can again profitably compare Tertullian's use of this method with that of his predecessors, allowing us to see the effects of Tertullian's particular context on his interpretation of Scripture and his understanding of the Spirit.[47] The key work in which Tertullian makes his most explicit and significant use of prosopological exegesis is his treatise *Against Praxeas* (ca. 210), in which he delivers a passionate rejection of what the literature calls modalistic monarchianism, a theological movement characterized by the belief that Father, Son, and Spirit are simply different modes or aspects of the one divine person. While its proponents held that this understanding was necessary to reconcile the divinity of

43. On North African Christianity, see Decret, *North Africa*; Burns and Jensen, *Roman Africa*.

44. For an overview of Tertullian's life and writings, see Dunn, *Tertullian*, 3–11.

45. See further Morgan-Wynne, *Holy Spirit*, 226–51.

46. For summaries of Tertullian's pneumatology and its significance, see, e.g., Thiselton, *Holy Spirit*, 178–83; Barnes, "Beginning and End," 184–86; Wilhite, "Spirit of Prophecy," 45–71.

47. On Tertullian's reliance on Justin and Irenaeus, see Evans, *Praxeas*, 31; Waszink, "Tertullian's Principles," 21.

Jesus with biblical monotheism, opponents such as Tertullian argued that this view in fact collapsed the distinctions between the members of the Godhead.[48] This treatise is also noteworthy for its positive statement of trinitarian theology, which would make a profound contribution to early Christian reflection on the subject; ironically, *Against Praxeas* is also thoroughly influenced by Tertullian's Montanist persuasions, which were later deemed heretical.[49] Specifically, then, we will need to consider what this pivotal, paradoxical text contributes concerning our study of prosopological exegesis from the person of the Spirit.

Tertullian's clear and succinct description of prosopological exegesis in *Prax.* 11 has received a fair amount of scholarly attention.[50] In this section of his treatise, Tertullian is attempting to demonstrate that Scripture makes a firm distinction between the Father and the Son. Thus, against the modalistic monarchians, Tertullian submits the following claim:

> All the Scriptures disclose both the demonstration and the distinction of the Trinity; from them also is deduced our rule: the person speaking and the person spoken to cannot be considered one and the same, because neither perversity nor deceit are consistent with God, so that, although it was himself to whom he was speaking, nevertheless he speaks to another and not to his own self.[51]

The language of identifying the speaking "persons" (*personae* in Tertullian's Latin being the equivalent of the Greek *prosōpa*) clearly marks this section as appealing to the person-centered reading strategy that we call prosopological exegesis. Tertullian then goes on to give examples of prosopological speech from the Father, the Son, and the Spirit (to which we will return shortly), concluding with the following statement summarizing his approach to prosopological exegesis:

> Thus in these passages, however few, the distinction of the Trinity is clearly set forth. For there is the Spirit himself who speaks,

---

48. On modalistic monarchianism, sometimes also known as Sabellianism or patripassionism, see further Evans, *Praxeas*, 6–18; Kelly, *Early Christian Doctrines*, 115–26.

49. On the trinitarian theology of *Against Praxeas* and its significance, see Osborn, *Tertullian*, 133–36; McGowan, "Tertullian and the Trinity," 61–81; McCruden, "Monarchy and Economy," 325–37. On the influence of Montanism on Tertullian's trinitarian theology, see especially McGowan, "Tertullian and the 'Heretical' Origins," 437–57.

50. See Andresen, "Zur Entstehung," 18–25; Slusser, "Exegetical Roots," 464–66; Bates, *Hermeneutics*, 185–86.

51. *Prax.* 11.4; all translations of *Against Praxeas* are mine unless otherwise noted.

the Father to whom he speaks, and the Son of whom he speaks. Likewise the rest, which are spoken sometimes by the Father concerning the Son or to the Son, sometimes by the Son concerning the Father or to the Father, sometimes by the Spirit, establish each person as distinct.[52]

What is particularly fascinating about this passage is how it complements Tertullian's earlier statement about prosopological exegesis in *Prax.* 11; whereas in the first instance Tertullian seems to suggest that his belief in the Trinity is the justification for his prosopological reading of Scripture, he here appears to argue that the doctrine of the Trinity is in fact derived from his prosopological interpretation. Tertullian must therefore imagine some kind of hermeneutical spiral, with his trinitarian beliefs and his person-centered reading of Scripture mutually informing one another.[53] We turn now to examine Tertullian's application of this method to the person of the Spirit.

Tertullian's Portrayal of the Spirit as a *Persona*

In the middle of this key chapter of *Against Praxeas*, having presented examples of the prosopological speech of the Father and the Son (*Prax.* 11.5–6), Tertullian now turns to the speech he attributes to the person of the Spirit:

> Consider also the Spirit speaking from a third person concerning the Father and the Son: *The Lord said to my Lord: Sit at my right hand, until I make your enemies a footstool for your feet* [Ps 110:1]. Again through Isaiah: *Thus says the Lord to my Lord Christ* [Isa 45:1]. Likewise through the same prophet, to the Father concerning the Son: *Lord, who has believed our report, and to whom is the arm of the Lord revealed? We have announced concerning him: like a young boy, like a root in a thirsty land, also there was no beauty or glory of his* [Isa 53:1–2].[54]

Tertullian, relative to his predecessors Justin and Irenaeus, has done a couple of very significant things here. First, Tertullian explicitly names

52. *Prax.* 11.9–10. On this and the preceding passage from *Prax.* 11, see further Hughes, *Trinitarian Testimony*, 157–61.

53. Cf. Slusser, "Exegetical Roots," 476: "It is difficult to say which came first, the exegesis of experience or the exegesis of Scripture."

54. *Prax.* 11.7–8. On this passage, see further Hughes, *Trinitarian Testimony*, 163–67.

the Spirit as a distinct divine person in the context of his functioning as a primary speaking agent, something that was present but not as clear in the earlier authors.[55] For Tertullian, though, the Spirit is succinctly described as speaking "from a third person (*persona*)," which is again an explicit invocation of an appeal to a person-centered reading strategy. Second, whereas his predecessors used prosopological exegesis from the Spirit to provide evidence of the Spirit testifying to the divinity and lordship of the Father and the Son, this theme is no longer present in Tertullian's surrounding interpretation (though it may still be inferred from the quotations themselves, with the Spirit calling the Father and the Son both "Lord");[56] rather, Tertullian is simply concerned to demonstrate the distinctiveness of each divine person.[57]

Third, and most importantly for our purposes, Tertullian redefines the very notion of personhood that is applied to the Spirit. As we have seen, Justin and Irenaeus used the Greek term *prosōpon* to describe the "character" or "person" participating in the divine theodrama, a word that would have had clear overtones from the world of theater. Tertullian, though, writing in Latin, uses the word *persona* as a logical stand-in for the Greek *prosōpon*, albeit with a different set of connotations. As Eric Osborn has argued, the term *persona* is used here in the sense of "the effective manifestation of a distinct being."[58] Likewise, Ernest Evans claims that *persona* is ultimately grounded in the legal sphere to refer to "one who has an existence and a status and rights of his own as well as relations and obligations in respect of others."[59] In other words, Tertullian has taken the notion of divine personhood out of the realms of theater or literature and into a portrayal (albeit still operating to some extent metaphorically) of the inner life of the Godhead.[60]

55. For this reason, scholars looking for examples of the Spirit's prosopological speech tend to start here, with the contributions of Justin and Irenaeus generally sidelined; see, e.g., Andresen, "Zur Entstehung," 18–25; Rondeau, *Les commentaires patristiques*, 30–34; Slusser, "Exegetical Roots," 464–65.

56. As for the quotations themselves, it is interesting that Tertullian keeps the quotation of Ps 110:1 but trades Ps 45:6–7 and Gen 19:24 for Isa 45:1 and Isa 53:1–2.

57. As will be detailed in the next chapter of this book, Tertullian explores the theme of the trinitarian testimony of the Spirit more through the lens of the Spirit's function in revealing the divine economy. In any event, as in Justin and Irenaeus, only the Spirit so testifies; see Hughes, *Trinitarian Testimony*, 167–81.

58. Osborn, *Tertullian*, 137.

59. Evans, *Praxeas*, 14.

60. McGowan, "Tertullian and the Trinity," 67: "Tertullian thus takes diversity of divine speech in scripture as a real indication of the differentiated reality of divine persons."

Tertullian's language in this passage signals that shift; whereas Justin and Irenaeus primarily portrayed the Spirit as speaking in the character of either the Father or the Son, and made consistent reference to the presence of the human prophet, Tertullian portrays each divine person as fully distinct and does not allude to the prophet in any way. Thus, in both the term *persona* itself as well as in the way in which Tertullian introduces the biblical quotations, Tertullian is portraying the Spirit as a distinct divine person.

Lest there be any doubt about this shift, a further consideration of Tertullian's context is instructive. Given that Tertullian was writing against the modalistic monarchians, who believed that Father, Son, and Spirit were different forms of the one divine being, the traditional language of prosopological exegesis, with its association with "masks" and "characters," could have been easily exploited by his opponents. Tertullian therefore had no choice but to set his use of prosopological exegesis, so crucial for providing biblical justification for his doctrine of distinction within the Godhead, on a different foundation. In so doing, Tertullian has endowed the Spirit with a more substantial degree of personhood than had either of his predecessors.[61] The Spirit would be, henceforth, a distinct divine person.

Interestingly, while Tertullian's use of prosopological exegesis greatly strengthened the case for the Spirit's distinct personhood, it also diminished one key aspect of the Spirit's work. In his prosopological reading of Old Testament passages spoken by the figure of Wisdom (e.g., Prov 8:22), Irenaeus had identified this Wisdom as none other than the Spirit, thus fashioning a robust theology of the Spirit as Creator.[62] Tertullian, however, takes such passages concerning Wisdom to be referring not to the Spirit but to the Son.[63] It appears that the modalistic monarchians identified God with Spirit, such that the Son is the union of the Spirit of God and human flesh; therefore, to combat this claim, Tertullian takes those Old Testament passages that portrayed the Spirit as Creator to be speaking of the Son before his incarnation, such that Spirit refers to the divine, pre-incarnate part of Christ.[64] As Michel Barnes summarizes, "In short, the exegetical basis

---

Cf. Prestige, *God in Patristic Thought*, 159.

61. At the very least, Tertullian is making explicit what was, at most, conceivably implicit in the writings of Justin and Irenaeus.

62. Cf. *Haer.* 4.20.3; see further Barnes, "Beginning and End," 178; Blowers, *Drama of the Divine Economy*, 113–18, 286–307; Briggman, *Irenaeus*, 129–31.

63. Cf. *Prax.* 6–7; see further Barnes, "Beginning and End," 183–84.

64. Barnes, "Beginning and End," 180. Barnes thus favors the term "Spirit-Monarchianism" for this Western form of monarchianism and the term "Spirit Christology" for

for a theology of the Holy Spirit is under-cut: the key passages are now understood to refer to the pre-existent Son in support of a theology of His distinct and personal existence before and during His Incarnation."[65] Thus, while this exegetical strategy may have been useful in combating modalistic monarchianism, it diminished the significance of the Spirit and no doubt played into the subordination that characterized Tertullian's trinitarian theology, as we will see in the next chapter of this book.

Conclusion

In this chapter, we have observed that Justin, Irenaeus, and Tertullian each made use of an ancient person-centered reading strategy that scholars have termed prosopological exegesis. Looking specifically at how each of these early Christian exegetes understood the relation of the Spirit to prosopological exegesis, we found evidence of both continuity and discontinuity. For Justin, the Spirit primarily (as he participates in the Logos) functions as the inspiring secondary agent that allowed the prophet to slip into different theodramatic roles, though we did identify instances in which Justin conceived of the Spirit as capable of speaking theodramatically as a primary speaking agent, that is, as his own "person" (*prosōpon*). Irenaeus largely echoed the approach of his predecessor, although his emerging trinitarian theology allowed him to more clearly portray the Spirit as a distinct theodramatic person. For both Justin and Irenaeus, the Spirit's prosopological speech was interpreted as providing testimony to the divinity and lordship of the Father and the Son. Tertullian, however, as heir to this tradition made some important changes. On the one hand, Tertullian's conception of "person" (*persona*) brought this notion out of the theatrical or literary spheres in which the language of prosopological exegesis had its origin, and instead used it in order to make a statement about the internal dynamics of the Godhead; the Spirit was, therefore and henceforth, a distinct divine person, not just in a literary or theodramatic sense but in something approaching an ontological one. On the other, though, Tertullian severed the link between prosopological exegesis and the Spirit's provision of divine testimony, leading to a decline in this theme over the subsequent century.[66]

Tertullian's response: "Western Spirit Christology is properly so-called only after distinctions of 'spirit' are worked out" as in Tertullian's time (ibid., 181 n. 31).

65. Barnes, "Beginning and End," 181.

66. On this point, see further Hughes, *Trinitarian Testimony*, 194–202.

It was nevertheless the case that this language of divine "persons" would be decisive in the formulation of Nicene theology. In the Latin West, the language of three *personae* would serve as the foundation of the understanding of God as Trinity. In the Greek-speaking East, however, the language of *prosōpon* would fall out of favor in the wake of the conflict over Sabellianism, which maintained that the one divine person simply played different roles at different times in salvation history.[67] The terminology that Basil of Caesarea used in discussing the Sabellian error was significant. According to Basil, they believed that God was only one *hypostasis* who took on different *prosōpa*, which here has the original theatrical sense of "roles" or "masks."[68] Thus, to the extent that the word was tainted by the specter of modalism, it would be *hypostasis* that would be the Eastern term of choice for distinct existence within the Godhead. Still, as Bates argues, "it was the Monarchian crisis itself that compelled the early church to reflect more precisely on the quality of individuality of the divine persons presupposed by prosopological exegesis, to extract the prosopa metaphor embedded in the exegetical technique, and to generalize toward individual divine persons."[69] Thus, though scholarship has not traditionally been attentive to the importance of this person-centered reading strategy for the development of trinitarian theology, it is nevertheless the case that the metaphor of one substance in three persons would become the "normative grammar" for orthodox Christian understanding of the Trinity.[70] Justin, surprisingly, emerges from this account as the innovator and progenitor of this decisive contribution to the Christian doctrine of God and the Spirit's place within it.

Gazing again at the mosaic of early Christian pneumatology, we are struck by how the next major tile in the section portraying the Spirit's unique divine personhood, representing the Spirit's prosopological speech as a primary speaking agent, is so carefully aligned with those tiles representing the Spirit's provision of divine testimony and the Christianization of the Spirit with respect to the Old Testament. When the colors of those previous tiles are combined with the pattern that emerges from a prosopological reading of Scripture, it turns out that there is both a surprising continuity and significant development from these previously overlooked tiles representing

---

67. Prestige, *God in Patristic Thought*, 113.

68. Cf. *Ep.* 236.6; see further Behr, *Nicene Faith*, 2:299.

69. Bates, *Birth*, 36 n. 62.

70. Thus, we can agree with Bates (*Birth*, 22) that prosopological exegesis was "irreducibly essential to the birth of the Trinity." See Hughes, *Trinitarian Testimony*, 206–13.

early pre-Nicene pneumatology. This tile glows with a strong sense of the Spirit's personhood and, like the tiles placed before it, was crafted from the raw material of Scripture and set in place with the adhesive of the continued experience of the Spirit in the Christian community. At the edge of this new tile, however, the pattern representing prosopological exegesis begins to lose its coloring that represents divine testimony; rather, we see that this color begins to bleed into a new pattern found in a neighboring tile. This adjacent tile represents the Spirit's role in revealing the divine economy, a function of the Spirit that we will explore in the next chapter of this book.

CHAPTER 5

The Spirit and the Divine Economy

In the third century of the Common Era, new currents in Platonic philosophy transformed the religious landscape of the late ancient Mediterranean world. As Heidi Marx-Wolf has demonstrated, the Platonists of this period placed great emphasis on defining and ordering the spiritual realm; in Marx-Wolf's analysis, these philosophers engaged in a "comprehensive philosophical project" that sought to create "complex discourses that mapped and ordered the realm of spirits in more systematic, universal terms."[1] According to Marx-Wolf, these "taxonomic discourses" were not abstract academic exercises, but ultimately served the purpose of promoting these philosophers' own influence and authority while discrediting their opponents.[2] One particularly popular line of argument for these philosophers was to claim that the deity that they worshipped was superior to the deities of rival religious groups, promising their followers access to a higher spiritual power than that on offer by others.[3]

It is in precisely this context that we can understand the competing claims of various groups that took the label of "Christian" to identify and rank a diverse array of heavenly beings. In this battle for religious authority and access to the supreme deity, the issue of the unity and diversity of God, and the role of the Holy Spirit in revealing that God, would come to be revealed as major flash points. Over the course of this chapter, then, we will examine how Christian writers of the late-second and third centuries appealed to the notion of the "divine economy" to set forth what would come to be identified as a fully trinitarian understanding of the Godhead, giving

1. Marx-Wolf, *Spiritual Taxonomies*, 38.

2. Marx-Wolf, *Spiritual Taxonomies*, 101.

3. Marx-Wolf, *Spiritual Taxonomies*, 122.

special attention to the function assigned to the Holy Spirit within that divine economy and to how the Spirit was understood in relation to the Father and the Son. As we will see, while this approach to the work of the Holy Spirit stood in continuity with some of the other pneumatological moves examined earlier in this book, it also moved early Christian conceptions of the Spirit in a new direction, helping further carve out a place and a role for the Spirit within the Godhead. For each of the three primary writers examined in this chapter—Irenaeus of Lyons, Tertullian of Carthage, and Origen of Alexandria—we will need to first assess their overall understanding of the divine economy and then, specifically, identify how the Spirit fits into that broader understanding. In so doing, we will find that the Spirit at last fully emerges as a distinct divine person even as the pneumatological advances that brought this about set up a series of further difficulties for subsequent Christian reflection on the person and work of the Spirit.

Irenaeus

As mentioned in the previous chapter of this book, Irenaeus of Lyons (ca. 135–200) wrote his magisterial *Against Heresies* (ca. 185) to refute the cosmological speculations of his various gnostic opponents. Anticipating the Neoplatonism of the third century, the gnostics were particularly concerned to construct a carefully delineated cosmos, in this case one in which dozens of lesser spirits, known as Aeons, were defined and ordered according to their degree of removal from the supreme deity. Generally speaking, the gnostics conceived of the creator god as one of these lesser spiritual beings who was in fact ignorant of the true Father God.[4] For Irenaeus, then, the challenge was to demonstrate how the right interpretation of Scripture (in this case, both Old and New Testaments) leads to the conclusion that there is only one God, in whom the Son is included alongside the Father. The basis of Irenaeus' response, to which we now turn, was his conception of the divine economy.

Irenaeus and the Divine Economy

The term "economy" (*oikonomia*) was commonly used in classical rhetoric to refer to the way in which the various pieces of a text are put together for

---

4. See further *Haer.* 1.2.1–5, 1.4.1–2; Lashier, *Irenaeus on the Trinity*, 32–36; Steenberg, *Irenaeus on Creation*, 22–27.

the purpose of proving its overall "hypothesis" (*hypothesis*). Scripture, therefore, has an economy that must be attended to in order to correctly interpret it. Beyond the world of rhetoric, the term "economy" was used by extension to describe a well-managed household or a well-arranged city. God, therefore, has an economy that is his well-ordered plan of providing salvation to human beings.[5] While Irenaeus was not the first Christian theologian to speak of the "divine economy," a term also used by the gnostics, Irenaeus did greatly develop this image, portraying God as a wise architect drafting the plans for salvation.[6] This allowed Irenaeus to provide a counter-narrative to the gnostic story of the (physical) problem with the human condition and the (spiritual) means of salvation, instead tracing how God's single purpose was carried throughout history.[7] His justification for his view of the divine economy was grounded in the "canon of truth" (*kanōn tēs alētheias*) or "rule of faith" (*regula fidei*), which summarized the content or plot of the Scriptures in a trinitarian or christological fashion.[8] Thus, if the rule of faith sets out the narrative content of Scripture, the economy describes the manner or sequence in which that plot is arranged.

Quite interestingly, Irenaeus specifies the purpose of this divine economy when he describes the reason why God created human beings in the first place. As he argues in book 4 of his *Against Heresies*, "in the beginning, it was not as if God, needing a human being, formed Adam, but rather so that he might have someone on whom he might bestow his benefits." Simply put, these benefits are nothing less than that "we may participate in his glory."[9] Through the Son's work of "recapitulation" (*anakephalaiōsis*), in which Christ culminates in himself the entire divine economy, humanity is reconstituted in a new and perfected form, able to enter into full communion with God.[10] Irenaeus' understanding of the divine economy, therefore, centers upon the process by which God is progressively leading

5. For a further discussion of the term "economy" and its background in antiquity, see Briggman, "Literary and Rhetorical Theory," 517–23; Grant, *Irenaeus*, 49–50; Osborn, *Irenaeus*, 74, 79.

6. See *Haer.* 4.14.2. The term can be found in the New Testament itself at Eph 1:10 and Eph 3:9, as well as in Ignatius and Justin. See further Behr, *Asceticism and Anthropology*, 33–85.

7. See further Blowers, *Drama of the Divine Economy*, 82–86.

8. On the *regula fidei* in Irenaeus, see Ferguson, *Rule of Faith*, 3–6, 17–19.

9. *Haer.* 4.14.1. Translations from *Against Heresies* are mine unless otherwise noted.

10. On recapitulation, see further Osborn, *Irenaeus*, 97–140; Blowers, *Drama of the Divine Economy*, 87–90; cf. *Haer.* 1.10.1, 5.1.1.

humanity into greater degrees of participation in God's own self, a process that extends across both this life and the next. With this broader context in mind, we can now turn to Irenaeus' conception of the Spirit's role within this divine economy.

Irenaeus and the Spirit in the Divine Economy

The Spirit, according to Irenaeus, has a critical role to play in the divine economy. Not only does the Spirit give life, in both this world and the next,[11] but the Spirit also, through all of salvation history, has had the function of preparing redeemed humanity for eternal life.[12] Irenaeus' clearest statement of this theme is found in book 4 of *Against Heresies*, in the midst of a discussion on the nature of a true spiritual disciple:

> For all things are evident to him: a complete faith in one God Almighty, from whom are all things . . . and in the Spirit of God, who furnishes the knowledge of the truth and who has made known the economies of the Father and the Son according to which he was present for the human race in every generation, as the Father wills.[13]

This very important passage has three key components. First, the Spirit "furnishes the knowledge of the truth." This clearly appropriates the Johannine motif of the Spirit leading Christians into the knowledge of the truth (cf. John 16:13). Second, the "truth" in view in this particular context is then specified as the knowledge of the workings of the divine economy, as handed down from the apostles via apostolic succession and preserved in Scripture (*Haer.* 4.33.8).[14] For Irenaeus, this knowledge of the divine economy has primarily to do with the fact that the Spirit reveals one God across all of Scripture, a God in which both the Creator and the Word subsist.[15] Third, the Spirit has been "present for the human race in all generations," connecting the Spirit's past activity to the Spirit's present work of enabling believers to share in the fullness of the divine life. Like the Old Testament

11. See further Behr, *Asceticism and Anthropology*, 86–115; Briggman, *Irenaeus*, 148–81.

12. Prior to the Christian era, this work of the Spirit included the inspiration of the prophets (*Haer.* 4.14.2) and the incarnation (*Haer.* 4.20.5); cf. Morgan-Wynne, *Holy Spirit*, 197.

13. *Haer.* 4.33.7. On this passage, see further Hughes, *Trinitarian Testimony*, 137–41.

14. See Morgan-Wynne, *Holy Spirit*, 211.

15. On the Word's role in the divine economy, see further *Haer.* 4.33.15.

prophets, Christians experience the Spirit so that they receive "that necessary discipline and training in order that [they] might be received into the future glory of God."[16] As the "Spirit of truth" (*Haer.* 4.35.2; cf. John 16:13), the Spirit is uniquely equipped for this role, for not only does the Spirit possess full truth, but he also possesses perfect knowledge, having always been present with God (*Haer.* 4.33.7). Believers have access to this Spirit through baptism (*Epid.* 41–42), by which they experience new life and new relationship with God (*Epid.* 6–7).[17] As Morgan-Wynne summarizes, "the Spirit is the agent of actualizing the risen Lord's presence in the believer," leading us to conclude that a conscious awareness of the Spirit's indwelling presence, and not merely an intellectual understanding, was a central part of how Irenaeus understood the concept of "knowing God."[18] After death, then, the believer can be confident of even more intimate communion with God, with the Spirit resurrecting the bodies of Christians to participate in eternal life with God (*Haer.* 3.24.1, 5.36.2).[19]

This account of the Spirit's role in revealing the divine economy has important connections to other themes examined in this book and sets up some significant ramifications. The first thing we need to appreciate is how Irenaeus' depiction of the Spirit's role in revealing the divine economy builds upon prior conceptions of the Spirit's divine testimony and the Spirit's prosopological speech. As we saw in the previous chapter of this book, Irenaeus used prosopological exegesis to portray the Spirit as speaking through the words of Scripture to testify to the lordship and divinity of the Father and the Son, something that I termed trinitarian testimony. Now, though, we can glimpse how Irenaeus has clarified (with respect to his predecessor Justin) that the Spirit's function as a primary speaking agent with respect to Scripture is in fact rooted in his broader conception of the work of the Holy Spirit in the divine economy. Putting this all together, Irenaeus' point is that the Spirit's provision of trinitarian testimony, recorded on the pages of Scripture as a window into the divine life of the triune God, is in fact precisely what is in view when we think of the Spirit preparing humanity to share in the life of the Godhead, which is the ultimate end of

16. Morgan-Wynne, *Holy Spirit*, 198, with reference to *Haer.* 4.20.8.

17. Morgan-Wynne, *Holy Spirit*, 199–205.

18. Morgan-Wynne, *Holy Spirit*, 206. This sense of the indwelling Spirit was likely manifested in the continued exercise of spiritual gifts such as prophecy and healing among Christians; see further Morgan-Wynne, *Holy Spirit*, 209–10.

19. Morgan-Wynne, *Holy Spirit*, 206.

the Spirit's revelation of the divine economy. In other words, if *Haer.* 4.14.1 gives the goal of the divine economy and *Haer.* 4.33.7 discloses the Spirit's role within that economy, *Haer.* 3.6.1 provides the means by which the Spirit is even now beginning to realize that goal.

The second thing that warrants our careful attention is how Irenaeus' understanding of the Spirit's role in the divine economy is inextricably linked with debates over the right interpretation of the Old Testament. Whereas Irenaeus' gnostic opponents sought to jettison the Old Testament, Irenaeus insists on the continued authority of the Old Testament because the Spirit who inspired the Hebrew prophets is in fact the same Spirit who is operative in the church age.[20] The Spirit's relationship to the Old Testament is thus seen on both the macro level of prophetic inspiration as well as on the micro level of prosopological exegesis in the Spirit's capacity as a primary speaking agent; both levels have the same end-goal, which is to point to Christ. More specifically, the notion of the Spirit's perfect knowledge of God, so central to Irenaeus' justification of the Spirit's role in revealing the divine economy, is in fact deeply rooted in Irenaeus' interpretation of the Old Testament. As noted in the previous chapter, as opposed to the vast majority of early Christian writers, Irenaeus understood the character of Wisdom in the book of Proverbs to be referring not to Christ but to the Holy Spirit. Quoting Prov 3:19–20, 8:22–25, and 8:27–31, Irenaeus claims that "Wisdom also, which is the Spirit, was present with [the Father], anterior to all creation."[21] The Spirit is therefore uniquely equipped for the task of revealing the divine economy on account of his perfect knowledge of God.

The third point that needs to be made is that Irenaeus' view of the Spirit and the divine economy is in fact deeply connected to his understanding of who truly possesses the Spirit. For Irenaeus, the truly spiritual disciple not only has faith in the Spirit who reveals the divine economy (*Haer.* 4.33.7), but also "receives the Spirit of God, who, from the beginning in all the dispensations of God, was present with human beings, and has announced the future, and has revealed the present, and explains the past."[22] As we have seen throughout this book, the possession of the Spirit is the *sine qua non* of Christian identity. What Irenaeus is here claiming is

20. See further Hughes, *Trinitarian Testimony*, 142–44. Here we should recall that the entirety of *Haer.* 4.20–35, in which this discussion of the Spirit is located, is devoted to demonstrating the harmony of the Old and New Testaments.

21. *Haer.* 4.20.3 (trans. *ANF*); see Briggman, *Irenaeus*, 129–31.

22. *Haer.* 4.33.1 (trans. Briggman, *Irenaeus*, 153); see Morgan-Wynne, *Holy Spirit*, 207–8.

that the person who "receives" or possesses the Holy Spirit is none other than the person who rightly understands the divine economy, which as noted above includes acceptance of the authority of the Spirit-inspired Old Testament.[23] Possession of the Spirit, therefore, is not only manifested in charismatic gifts or the fruit of the Spirit, but in right theology, in accepting the truth about God that the Spirit has revealed. To bring this back to the discussion of the insights of Marx-Wolf from the beginning of this chapter, Irenaeus is thus offering access to a Holy Spirit who in turn provides access, now only in part but later in full, to the triune God, thus bolstering his own religious authority.[24]

The fourth and final conclusion we need to draw is that Irenaeus' particular depiction of the Spirit as the one who reveals the divine economy set up future debates concerning the full deity of the Spirit. As detailed above, Irenaeus has made a clear case for the eternality, and therefore the divinity, of the Holy Spirit by drawing on the figure of Wisdom in Proverbs to cast the Spirit as an eternal person who was, along with the Son, one of the two "hands of God" in creation.[25] However, the citation of Prov 8:22 is inherently problematic for any claim to full divinity insofar as Wisdom speaks of having been "created" by the Lord. Though Anthony Briggman argues that this "should not be taken as revealing Irenaeus' understanding of, or even interest in, the generation of the Spirit," it is nevertheless the case that Irenaeus never offers an explanation for how the Spirit coexists with God, which certainly leaves him open to a challenge on this basis.[26] This, then, will have to be clarified by later writers who will insist on the full divinity of the Holy Spirit.

In summary, therefore, Irenaeus more clearly presents the Spirit as divine—having a distinct identity and function with respect to the other divine persons—than was the case in the New Testament, Barnabas, or

---

23. Morgan-Wynne, *Holy Spirit*, 211: "There is a twofold line of approach: the Spirit has produced the faith held by the church throughout the world, while those who adhere to such a faith clearly are led by the Spirit."

24. See further Hughes, *Trinitarian Testimony*, 144–45.

25. On the Son and the Spirit as the "hands of God" in creation, see further Blowers, *Drama of the Divine Economy*, 113–18, 286–307; Briggman, *Irenaeus*, 104–26.

26. Briggman, *Irenaeus*, 130. As Briggman continues, "In contrast to his comments on the generation of the Logos in *AH* 2, at no time does Irenaeus explain his conception of the production of the Spirit. In fact, he gives no indication that he considers it important to verbalize an account of the Spirit's production or that he even has an account that he could verbalize." See also Barnes, "Irenaeus's Trinitarian Theology," 94–96.

Justin. As we will see, as was the case concerning prosopological exegesis, Irenaeus' successor Tertullian both extends and transforms Irenaeus' understanding of the divine economy and the Spirit's role within it.

Tertullian

As explored in the previous chapter of this book, Tertullian of Carthage (ca. 160–215) wrote his treatise *Against Praxeas* (ca. 210) to combat the threat of modalistic monarchianism, which portrayed Father, Son, and Spirit as different manifestations of the one God. In writing this work, however, Tertullian was also motivated to defend the New Prophecy, later termed Montanism after one of its founders, which believed in the continuing work of the Paraclete of the Fourth Gospel in providing continuing, ecstatic revelation.[27] It is in this overall context, therefore, that we must locate Tertullian's distinct vision of the divine economy, and particularly the role of the Spirit within it.

Tertullian and the Divine Economy

Following his predecessor Irenaeus, Tertullian set out a view of the divine economy as a means of rightly interpreting the "rule of faith" of Scripture and thus the overall plan or sequence of God's actions in salvation history. Tertullian helpfully summarizes his approach at the outset of his treatise *Against Praxeas*:

> In truth, as always—and now even more so, being better instructed by the Paraclete, the leader into all truth—we believe that there is indeed one only God, yet under this dispensation (or "economy"), that this one only God has also a Son, his Word, who proceeded from himself, by whom all things were made, and without whom nothing has been made, . . . who then, in accordance with his promise, sent from the Father the Holy Spirit, the Paraclete, the sanctifier of the faith of those who believe in the Father and the Son and the Holy Spirit. That this rule has come down from the beginning of the Gospel . . . he will prove . . . .[28]

27. On the influence of Montanism on Tertullian, see further Thiselton, *Holy Spirit*, 178–83. On the role of the Paraclete in Montanism, see Trevett, *Montanism*, 62–66.

28. *Prax.* 2.1–2. All translations of *Against Praxeas* are mine unless noted otherwise. In contrast to other published translations, I take the Paraclete as the subject of the verb *probabit* given the prior context and the fact that this is an active verb (a normal transitive

Like Irenaeus, then, Tertullian sets out a vision of the divine economy that, following the rule of faith, distinguishes between the activities of Father, Son, and Spirit in the working out of God's salvific purposes. Where Tertullian makes a significant move beyond Irenaeus, however, is with his interest in detailing his understanding of how unity and diversity can coexist in the Godhead. After all, on the one hand, Tertullian needs to demonstrate that modalism does not adequately portray the distinction of the three divine persons, while on the other hand he needs to make sure he is not condemned as a tritheist. As Andrew McGowan summarizes, "Tertullian's main goal throughout [*Praxeas*] is to allay fears that the real existence of a second divine person would undermine the principle of a single divine power or *monarchia*."[29] Tertullian's solution to this dilemma was to offer various analogies for the Trinity that, in contrast to other such images circulating before and during his own time, encompass all three divine persons.[30] For instance, later in *Against Praxeas* Tertullian goes on to describe the Trinity in the following terms:

> For God brought forth the Word, as also the Paraclete teaches, as the root [brings forth] the tree, and the spring the river, and the sun the beam. For these also are the manifestations (or "projections") of those substances from which they proceed. . . . But where there is a second there are two, and where there is a third there are three. For the Spirit is third from God and the Son, as the fruit from the tree is third from the root, the stream from the river is third from the spring, and the apex of the beam is third from the sun. Nothing, however, is alienated from the source from which it derives its own properties. In this way the Trinity, flowing down from the Father by intertwined and connected degrees, does not impede the monarchy while it protects the condition of the economy.[31]

As the last sentence of this excerpt makes clear, Tertullian is offering this analogy for the Trinity in the context of his defense of the divine

---

verb should have a passive ending when being used impersonally, as other translations take it). This heightens the Montanist character of Tertullian's argument, but we must be wary of helping Tertullian come across as more "orthodox" than his writings actually suggest. On this passage, see further Hughes, *Trinitarian Testimony*, 182–83.

29. McGowan, "Tertullian and the 'Heretical' Origins," 443.

30. For earlier binitarian images involving only Father and Son, see Justin, *Dial.* 61.2, 128.3; Tatian, *Or. Graec.* 5.4; Hippolytus, *Noet.* 11; for an image involving only Father and Spirit, see Athenagoras, *Leg.* 10.4. See further McGowan, "Tertullian and the Trinity," 72–74.

31. *Prax.* 8.5, 8.7. On this passage, see further Hughes, *Trinitarian Testimony*, 183–86.

economy. As we saw above, Irenaeus was not interested in attempting an explanation of the generation of the Spirit or the Spirit's place in the Godhead. Now, however, the conflict with modalistic monarchianism has forced Tertullian to innovate in precisely this way. This image, then, is how Tertullian wants us to understand God as "Trinity" (*Trinitas*, with Tertullian being the one who coined this phrase), existing as "one substance" and "three persons" (*Prax.* 2.4).[32] This analogy warrants our further attention to the following three points.

First, Tertullian has subtly redefined the divine economy with respect to Irenaeus' earlier definition. Whereas Irenaeus focused on how God has revealed himself through the story of creation and redemption, Tertullian instead uses metaphors like this (among others) to make a statement about the nature of *God's own inner life*, which aligns with what we observed about Tertullian's use of the term *persona* in the previous chapter of this book.[33] As Kevin McCruden has argued, "Tertullian may have feared that if he had presented the economy in the more traditional historical manner he might have left an opening for his monarchian opponents to argue that the economy properly signifies the unfolding of the Father in the guise of the Son and the Holy Spirit."[34] In any event, Tertullian has moved us to a view of the economy that, while still in the realm of metaphor, nevertheless intends to convey truth concerning the *internal* relations among Father, Son, and Spirit.[35]

Second, Tertullian here introduces a new vocabulary for conceiving of the nature of the Trinity. As this passage makes clear, the Spirit is "third from God." In ranking the Spirit third within the Godhead, Tertullian appeals to the notion of "order" (*gradus*; cf. *Prax.* 2.4, 4.1) within the triune God.[36] On the one hand, this language owes more to the philosophy of the ancient world than to anything within the pre-existing Judeo-Christian tradition; indeed, for Michel René Barnes, this marks an embrace of "other theological superstructures" and therefore "an alternative grammar for

32. The technical terms Tertullian uses are *substantia* and *personae*.

33. McGowan, "Tertullian and the Trinity," 65: "Tertullian's economy is not the way God is revealed in history, but the self-disposition of God—rather more the 'immanent' Trinity of later theology than the 'economic.'"

34. McCruden, "Monarchy and Economy," 336.

35. Of course, in so doing, Tertullian has also redefined the notion of the divine monarchy; see McCruden, "Monarchy and Economy," 328–30.

36. On the meaning of *gradus* as combining elements of position, progression, and rank, see Rankin, "Tertullian's Vocabulary," 18–20.

theology of the Holy Spirit" at the expense of abandoning earlier views of the Spirit derived from Judaism.[37] On the other hand, however, the continuity between Irenaeus and Tertullian, with respect to both their use of prosopological exegesis and their views of the divine economy, should caution us against too firmly dividing these two early Christian exegetes into different "stages" of pneumatological development.

Third, this formulation of Tertullian sets up a problem for later trinitarian theologians: subordinationism. Part of the issue here is that Tertullian did not maintain that God has existed as Trinity for all eternity; rather, originally the one divine substance was undifferentiated.[38] Specifically regarding the Holy Spirit, McGowan notes that "the clearest indication that the Holy Spirit is a third person prior to creation or incarnation comes in Tertullian's exegesis of divine plural statements from the creation narratives of the Old Testament."[39] Even here, however, Tertullian's reference to the Spirit as "in the Word" (*Prax.* 12.3) "seems to leave open the possibility that the Holy Spirit subsists in the Word or the Son at this point and emerges into a fuller personal existence only later, with incarnation or Pentecost."[40] This appears to be the most logical basis for Tertullian's claim that the Spirit proceeds *from* the Father *through* the Son (*Prax.* 4.1). Our study of prosopological exegesis from the *persona* of the Spirit seems to push against such a possibility, but it is fair to say that the precise nature or extent of the Spirit's personhood is somewhat underdeveloped by Tertullian. Having established this broader context, we can now examine how Tertullian conceived of the Spirit's role within this divine economy.

Tertullian and the Spirit in the Divine Economy

Like Irenaeus before him, Tertullian portrays the Spirit as revealing the divine economy to humanity. Drawing on the Johannine image of the Spirit as the Paraclete who leads believers into all truth, Tertullian describes the

37. Barnes, "Beginning and End," 170, 184–86.

38. McGowan, "Tertullian and the Trinity," 65–68, with reference to *Prax.* 7–9. "Tertullian does not regard the trinitarian arrangement of divine substance either as absolutely essential to the eternal being of God, or as merely or immediately related to the events of salvation history. Rather it emerges within a sort of divine history that is related to the work of creation, even though it largely precedes it" (ibid., 65). Thus I believe it is fair to still speak of Tertullian as having an "economic trinitarianism," to use the modern label.

39. McGowan, "Tertullian and the Trinity," 71, with reference to *Prax.* 12.3.

40. McGowan, "Tertullian and the Trinity," 71.

Spirit as instructing believers concerning a correct understanding of the divine economy, emphasizing both unity and diversity in the Godhead (*Prax.* 2.1–2).[41] To this end, at the conclusion of his *Against Praxeas*, Tertullian makes the following comment:

> [The Son], meanwhile, has poured out the gift he has received from the Father, the Holy Spirit, the third name of the divinity and the third degree of the majesty, the preacher of the one monarchy but also the interpreter of the economy, and, if anyone admits the words of his New Prophecy, also the leader into all truth which is in the Father and the Son and the Holy Spirit according to the Christian mystery.[42]

Concerning this key passage, we can make three important observations. First, Tertullian identifies the purpose of the Spirit to be guiding believers into a proper understanding of God as Trinity, echoing Irenaeus's earlier development of this same point. This theme was already introduced in the above quotation from *Prax.* 2.1–2, but here in *Prax.* 30.5 Tertullian confirms and further specifies the nature of the Spirit's instruction by giving the Spirit the titles of "the preacher of the one monarchy" and "the interpreter of the economy." Thus, the Spirit both proclaims God to be one and teaches that this monarchy encompasses multiple divine persons. Second, again as with Irenaeus, Tertullian alludes to John 16:13 in naming the Spirit as "the leader into all truth," with the truth in view again that related to the divine economy.[43] Though not specified here, there is little question that we are to understand the Spirit to be primarily carrying out this task by means of inspiring Scripture, in both the primary and secondary senses described above. Besides this, however, Tertullian undoubtedly also believed the Paraclete (the favored Montanist term for the Holy Spirit) instructed Christians in the mystery of the Trinity through direct revelation, as expressed in the prophetic utterances of the Montanist prophets.[44] This third

41. On the influence of the New Prophecy on Tertullian's understanding of the Spirit's work in this regard, see McGowan, "Tertullian and the 'Heretical' Origins," 451–53.

42. *Prax.* 30.5. On this passage, see further Hughes, *Trinitarian Testimony*, 188–89.

43. Cf. *Praesc.* 22.9–10; Morgan-Wynne, *Holy Spirit*, 236.

44. See again my translation of *Prax.* 2.1 above. These two forms of the Spirit's testifying work are interrelated; Tertullian's references to the direct revelations of the Paraclete via the New Prophets were probably understood as a means of "the illumination of Scripture" (so Rankin, "Tertullian's Vocabulary," 7). This calls to mind the prophetic teaching of the Spirit described in Hebrews; in fact, Hebrews seems to have been particularly attractive to the Montanists (so Trevett, *Montanism*, 131). See further Tertullian's

observation is of course where we see a clear break from what Tertullian had received from Irenaeus. While Irenaeus certainly believed in prophecy and spiritual gifts and appears to have been somewhat sympathetic to some elements of Montanism, he likely opposed its strict asceticism and rigor as well as its ecstatic, disorderly character.[45] In sum, then, though Tertullian's specific polemical context has sharpened the precision of his understanding of unity and diversity in the Godhead, and while his Montanist leanings clearly influenced his understanding of the Spirit's work, his account of the Spirit's role in revealing the divine economy is clearly in continuity with that of his predecessor Irenaeus.[46]

Extending our vision outward, two concluding points must be made to demonstrate the significance of Tertullian's pneumatology for the overall argument of this book. First, Tertullian unambiguously here portrays the Spirit as a distinct divine person. The battle with modalistic monarchianism, as we have seen above, led Tertullian to put forward an understanding of the Spirit's prosopological speech that moved the term *persona* out of the theatrical or literary realms and into that of the inner life of the Godhead. With the Spirit's revelation of the divine economy, we can observe the same impulse at work; the Spirit is given a distinct identity and function within the Trinity insofar as the Spirit testifies to the other divine persons. As David Rankin concludes, Tertullian "believed that the denial by Praxeas and his kind of the distinct identity of each of the persons of the Holy Trinity was tantamount to a denial of their existence."[47] Tertullian's solution to this problem, then, was to appeal to the Holy Spirit as the one who so testifies to the distinct identity of the Father and the Son. This had profound implications for his understanding of the Spirit insofar as "[the Spirit's] authority, as teacher and

---

description of such a prophetess in *An.* 9.

45. This judgment is supported by Eusebius' account at *Hist. eccl.* 5.1–4, which depicts the churches of Lyons and Vienne as sympathetic to the New Prophecy and Irenaeus as advocating for peace with the churches of Asia and Phrygia. See further Grant, *Irenaeus*, 6; Morgan-Wynne, *Holy Spirit*, 250; Marjanen, "Montanism," 194; Parvis, "Who Was Irenaeus?" 23. *Contra* Osborn, *Irenaeus*, 6, Irenaeus' critical words at *Haer.* 3.11.9 most likely do not have the Montanists in view (so Heine, "Role of the Gospel of John," 14). For further discussion of the reasons why Montanism was condemned, see Stewart-Sykes, "Original Condemnation," 9–18, emphasizing Montanism's rural origins; Marjanen, "Montanism," 184–212, emphasizing a variety of factors, including the ecstatic nature of its prophecy, its claims to authority, egalitarianism, and payment of salaries to leaders and teachers.

46. See again *Haer.* 4.33.7.

47. Rankin, "Tertullian's Vocabulary," 7.

director, would amount to nothing if his existence as a distinct being could not be guaranteed."[48] In sum, Rankin concludes, "it is, at least in part, the testimony of the Holy Spirit which establishes these distinctions and thus its own identity and authority."[49] Thus, the very nature of Tertullian's argument inevitably leads him to an understanding of the Spirit as a distinct divine person. Indeed, the underlying logic appears to run, only a third, fully distinct person sharing the same substance (*substantia*) would have the qualifications or authority to provide trinitarian testimony.[50]

Second, Tertullian's portrayal of the Spirit as a distinct divine person includes two elements that would pose difficulties for later Christian theologians. One of these problems, that of subordinationism, we have already encountered in our earlier discussion of Tertullian's analogies for the Trinity. Returning to *Prax.* 30.5, we have yet another reference to the Spirit as the third "degree" (*gradum*) of the being of God. As Rankin notes, "Here we have the suggestion of a hierarchy in the Godhead, which Tertullian is prepared to accept with the attendant risk of suggesting a notion of subordinationism, for he will do everything he possible [*sic*] can to avoid the greater dangers of modalism."[51] An additional problem, however, concerns the centrality of the New Prophecy for Tertullian's understanding of the Spirit. It was only after Tertullian came to fully embrace the teachings of Montanism that he put forward the conception of the Spirit that we have analyzed in this chapter; after all, *Against Praxeas*, a text foundational for later trinitarian theology, is motivated in large part to defend the New Prophecy against criticism.[52] Thus, Tertullian claims that the Spirit will reveal the truth of the divine economy only to the one who "accepts the words of his New Prophecy" (*Prax.* 30.5). To acknowledge Tertullian's view of the Trinity is to acknowledge the authority of the Paraclete, over both doctrine and practice.[53] We see the reality behind

48. Rankin, "Tertullian's Vocabulary," 8.

49. Rankin, "Tertullian's Vocabulary," 8.

50. As McGowan, "Tertullian and the Trinity," 77, points out, the third element in each of these sequences is the one "most concerned with ends or goals, and with human experience and participation." This lines up with Irenaeus' vision of the Spirit preparing humankind for participating in the life of the Godhead.

51. Rankin, "Tertullian's Vocabulary," 20.

52. As indicated in, e.g., *Prax.* 1.5; cf. *Prax.* 2.1–2, 30.5. See further McGowan, "Tertullian and the 'Heretical' Origins," 440–55.

53. McGowan, "Tertullian and the 'Heretical' Origins," 452: "For [Tertullian] the Paraclete is that aspect of God's being that turns theory into practice, linking and unifying

this when, for instance, Tertullian credits his aforementioned trinitarian images to the inspiration of the Paraclete (*Prax.* 8.5), suggesting that these images were in fact taken from one of the New Prophets' inspired utterances.[54] Following Timothy Barnes, then, we have little choice but to conclude that "Tertullian helped to rescue the Catholic Church from theological heresy precisely because he was a Montanist."[55]

Tertullian's legacy was, therefore, a complicated one. For one thing, even though in some respects we can speak of Tertullian having a "lower" pneumatology than Irenaeus, whether on account of his subordinationism or (as discussed in the previous chapter of this book) his decision to identify the Son as the subject of Old Testament texts that Irenaeus had previously associated with the Spirit,[56] in other respects we can fairly speak of Tertullian as having a "higher" pneumatology than did his predecessors. For another, given that Tertullian so closely linked the Spirit's roles in providing testimony to the other divine persons and revealing the divine economy with his Montanist beliefs, it is not surprising that Tertullian's immediate successors in the Latin tradition would de-emphasize these elements of the Spirit's work.[57] To this subject we will now briefly turn.

After Tertullian: Novatian and the Decline of the Spirit

Novatian of Rome (ca. 200–258), the next great trinitarian theologian in the West, provides us with an interesting lens through which to view Tertullian's legacy.[58] Like Tertullian, Novatian was a moral rigorist who clashed with the larger church and wrote a treatise against modalistic monarchianism. This treatise, *On the Trinity* (ca. 245), is a landmark in Western theology, building on the works of writers including Justin, Irenaeus, and, above all, Tertullian in constructing what Russell DeSimone calls "a Latin handbook

---

disciplina and *doctrina.*"

54. McGowan, "Tertullian and the 'Heretical' Origins," 445.

55. Barnes, *Tertullian*, 142.

56. On this latter point, see further Barnes, "Beginning and End," 180–84, referencing Tertullian's identification of Wisdom in Prov 8 as the Son.

57. On this topic, see further Hughes, *Trinitarian Testimony*, 194–202.

58. For an overview of the life of Novatian, see DeSimone, *Treatise of Novatian*, 21–36.

of dogma" that "brought the development of trinitarian theology to a certain conclusion for the pre-Augustinian period."[59]

In this treatise, Novatian follows Tertullian in opposing modalistic monarchianism through an appeal to the divine "economy" (the Latin *dispositio* being the equivalent of the Greek *oikonomia*).[60] The biggest advance that Novatian makes concerning the divine economy with respect to Tertullian is that he claims that the Son was eternally distinct from the Father; there has never been a time, he claims, when the Son was not the Son or the Father was not the Father (*Trin.* 31.3).[61] Within this economy, the Spirit is clearly subordinated to the Son (*Trin.* 16.3), though the nature of that subordination, and its implications for the debate over the mode of the Spirit's procession, is not entirely clear.[62] It might also be significant that nowhere in this treatise does Novatian affirm the distinct personal existence and divinity of the Spirit; only the Father and the Son are described as *personae* by Novatian.[63] While this surprising neglect may be tempered by the fact that Novatian's description of the work of the Spirit seems to presuppose the distinct divine personhood of the Spirit,[64] the precious little attention given to the Spirit in this treatise is nevertheless indicative of the Spirit's relative lack of importance for Novatian.

Novatian devotes only a single chapter to the Holy Spirit near the end of his treatise *On the Trinity*. Novatian's main focus here seems to be on demonstrating that the Spirit who presently endows believers with charismatic gifts, sanctifies them, and prepares them for immortality is in fact the same Spirit who inspired the Old Testament prophets and the New Testament apostles. To this end Novatian pulls together a wealth of biblical quotations that describe the person and work of the Holy Spirit. Among these quotations are the familiar passages from the Johannine Farewell Discourse, and thus the Spirit is the Paraclete, the "Spirit of Truth" (cf. John 16:13). However, where we would expect Novatian to follow Tertullian in unpacking this understanding in more detail by identifying the Spirit as

---

59. DeSimone, *Treatise of Novatian*, 8. This treatise was handed down with the title *On the Trinity* despite the fact that Novatian never uses the word "Trinity" in this writing.

60. References to the divine economy may be found in *Trin.* 3.1, 15.12, 18.10, 24.9.

61. See DeSimone, *Treatise of Novatian*, 43; Papandrea, *Novatian of Rome*, 33–34.

62. For further discussion, see DeSimone, "Holy Spirit," 371–76.

63. See Simonetti, "Il regresso," 657–59.

64. See DeSimone, "Holy Spirit," 364–65, 376–80; Papandrea, *Novatian of Rome*, 108–9.

the preacher of the monarchy or the interpreter of the economy, Novatian gives us only silence. The closest Novatian gets to any notion of the Spirit revealing the divine economy is his statement that the Spirit is the one who reveals divine things (*Trin.* 29.9), but even this in context likely only refers to the Spirit helping believers rightly understand Christ's life and work. There is, therefore, no indication that Novatian believed the Spirit reveals the divine economy, and therefore this idea of trinitarian testimony, which has been so central to the pneumatology studied so far in this book, is completely absent in Novatian's work.[65]

The best explanation for this is, of course, the residual taint of Tertullian's Montanism. Around 235 CE, the Asian bishops who gathered at the Synod of Iconium issued a condemnation of Montanism and its adherents. As a result, Montanism declined across the Christian world, including in the West.[66] Understandably, Novatian and other Western theologians, who were otherwise indebted to Tertullian, were eager to distance themselves from any hint of sympathy to Montanism. Given how inextricably connected Tertullian's argument concerning the Trinity was with his defense of the New Prophecy, if anything we should be surprised how much of Tertullian's trinitarian thought was retained by his successors. Thus, we should not be surprised to find that Novatian has diminished the work, if not also the person, of the Holy Spirit.

Indeed, this trajectory of pneumatological "decline" continued after the time of Novatian; subsequent writers in the Latin tradition do not discuss the relationship of the Spirit to the Father and the Son, and so the portrayal of the Spirit providing testimony to the other divine persons and revealing the divine economy fades from view. From the perspective of the Roman church, therefore, the Nicene Creed of 325, which simply posits belief in the Holy Spirit without reference to his divine personhood or any elaboration of his ministry, serves as a fitting close to the trajectory of early Christian pneumatology in the West after the time of

---

65. Nor do we find Novatian citing instances of the Spirit's prosopological speech, whether for the purpose of providing trinitarian testimony or otherwise; this is all the more surprising when we find the "two powers" texts of the Old Testament, from which Novatian draws the conclusion that Christ is "Lord" and "God," cited without any appeal to the work of the Spirit (as at *Trin.* 18.14, 26.4–7). As observed above, Tertullian began the process of severing the explicit link between prosopological exegesis and the trinitarian testimony of the Spirit, and with Novatian we find this link severed completely.

66. On the Synod of Iconium and its influence, see further Tabbernee, "Initiation/ Baptism," 923.

Tertullian. In the East, however, reflection on the Spirit's revelation of the divine economy continued to take place, thanks in large part to a single, towering figure: Origen.

Origen

Origen of Alexandria (ca. 185–255), by all accounts one of the most brilliant and prolific figures in all of pre-Nicene Christianity, serves as our final point of analysis in our discussion of the Spirit's revelation of the divine economy. Origen started his career in Alexandria, where he drew on the rich heritage of Alexandrian Christianity and his own training in literary studies to produce some of his most famous works, including his *On First Principles* (ca. 230), which will be the focus of this chapter.[67] Despite its attempt to clarify and bring unity around the apostolic teaching, this work of systematic theology would have significant repercussions for Origen, leading him to depart Alexandria for Caesarea and, three centuries later, resulting in him being anathematized as a heretic.[68] In our analysis of this work, which survives in its entirety only in the Latin translation of Rufinus and thus presents many interpretive challenges,[69] we will find the most complete presentation of Origen's dynamic pneumatology, focusing in particular on what Origen teaches concerning the Spirit's role in revealing the divine economy.[70] As we will see, Origen develops this theme in novel ways that extend beyond the views of the divine economy set forth previously by Irenaeus and Tertullian.[71]

---

67. On Origen's early life and his Alexandrian context, see further Heine, *Origen*, 1–61, 83–144; Trigg, *Origen: Bible and Philosophy*, 31–34; Behr, *Origen: On First Principles*, 1:xvii–xx.

68. Heine, *Origen*, 143–44.

69. See further Behr, *Origen: On First Principles*, 1:xx–xxiv.

70. For a full overview of Origen's pneumatology, see Thiselton, *Holy Spirit*, 183–87. Among many items of interest, Origen emphasizes that the Spirit's authority and dignity is seen in the Spirit's inclusion in the trinitarian baptismal formula (*Princ.* 1.3.2) and that possession of the Holy Spirit is required for salvation (*Princ.* 1.3.5).

71. According to Eusebius (*Hist. eccl.* 6.14.10), Origen went to Rome ca. 215, making it likely that he came into contact with the works of Irenaeus if not also of Tertullian. See Trigg, *Origen: Bible and Philosophy*, 76–80.

Origen and the Divine Economy

We saw above that Tertullian expanded his understanding of the divine economy to include not simply the way in which God is revealed in history but also the inner life or self-disposition of God. While Origen will likewise explore both of these topics, it is only the former that Origen describes as "economic."[72] Despite this shift in vocabulary, we will want to be attentive to what Origen says about what theologians term both the ontological (or immanent) Trinity and the economic Trinity before turning to the Spirit's role in revealing the divine economy, as understood in the broader sense of the term.

Starting, then, with Origen's treatment of God with respect to his divine nature, we must remember that, in *On First Principles*, Origen is synthesizing ideas from Scripture as well as Middle Platonism; the influence of the latter is seen in the title and the genre of the work, both of which are clearly indebted to the world of Middle Platonism.[73] Accordingly, when Origen sets out to describe the Trinity (a term Origen uses often, albeit without an explicit articulation of his doctrine on the subject),[74] he utilizes the Platonic idea of *hypostasis* to indicate distinct existence within the Trinity.[75] Likewise bringing together his interpretation of Scripture with the insights of Platonic philosophy, Origen argues that the three divine *hypostases*—Father, Son, and Spirit—are immaterial and eternally exist in a ranked order characteristic of the subordinationism that we have seen is so characteristic of pre-Nicene theology.[76] Where Origen's view of the Trinity goes beyond any of his predecessors—explicitly, at least—is his claim that the Son and the Spirit have *eternally existed* with the Father. Preceding a similar articulation by Novatian by about two decades, Origen's doctrine of the eternal generation of the other two divine *hypostases* rested on the

---

72. Cf., e.g., *Princ.* 1.2.1. Behr, *Origen: On First Principles*, 1:xxxix, in fact understands the structure of *On First Principles* as comprising two major cycles, focused first on "theology" proper (*Princ.* 1.1—2.3) and then on the "economy" (*Princ.* 2.4—3.6).

73. Widdicombe, *Fatherhood of God*, 9–10.

74. Heine, *Origen*, 137: "The totality of these references does not add up to anything like a complete doctrine of the Trinity in the work." It is possible that the frequency of the usage of this term owes more to Rufinus than Origen himself (so McDonnell, "Origen," 11), but the emphasis on God as "three and one" is clear regardless.

75. Outside of *On First Principles*, see *Comm. John* 2.10.75. On the term *hypostasis*, see further Ramelli, "Trinitarian Meaning of *Hypostasis*," 302–9, 316–25.

76. See further Trigg, *Origen*, 23–24.

presupposition that statements concerning the nature of God transcend human understandings of time.[77] As Peter Widdicombe summarizes, "For Origen what is said of God must eternally be true," and therefore God has always existed as Father, Son, and Spirit.[78]

Within this framework, therefore, we can examine Origen's specific statements about the nature of the Holy Spirit. The Spirit, Origen states clearly, is "an intellectual being and subsists and exists distinctly" (*Princ.* 1.1.3); here the Latin word translated "being," *subsistentia*, is presumably Rufinus' translation of the Greek *hypostasis*.[79] Like the Son, the Spirit has existed alongside the Father from before the beginning of creation:

> But up to the present time we have been able to find no passage in the holy Scriptures in which the Holy Spirit is said to be made or created, not even in the way that we have shown above that Solomon speaks of Wisdom, or the way in which expressions such as Life or Word or the other titles of the Son of God, which we have treated, are to be understood. *The Spirit of God*, therefore, who *moved upon the waters* [Gen 1:2], as it is written, in the beginning of the creation of the world, I think to be none other than the Holy Spirit, so far as I am able to understand.[80]

Thus, as opposed to all created beings, the Spirit exists eternally with the Father and the Son.[81] Interestingly, despite Origen's recognition of the Spirit's presence at creation, he ascribes the actual work of creation to the Son; like Tertullian, Origen identifies the Wisdom character of Prov 8 as the Son, not the Spirit.[82] That the Spirit would have no meaningful role in creation is just one example of how Origen attributes such a vast array of functions to the Son that the Spirit's distinctive role is quite circumscribed.[83] Part of the reason for this, perhaps, is that while Origen identifies the work of the Father and the Son as involving all of creation, the work of the Spirit, especially in regards to its gifting of the charisms, is only operative among

77. Cf. *Princ.* 1.3.4; see further McDonnell, "Origen," 12–15.

78. Widdicombe, *Fatherhood of God*, 69.

79. Cf. Behr, *Origen: On First Principles*, 1:29 n. 16; see also *Princ.* 1.3.1–2.

80. *Princ.* 1.3.3. All translations of *On First Principles* are from the edition of Behr.

81. Cf. *Princ.* 4.4.1; see further Tzamalikos, *Origen*, 25: "The idea is that there was no state in which the Son and the Holy Spirit did not exist together with the Father, since the very being of the Trinity is timeless."

82. See Behr, *Origen: On First Principles*, 1:lvi; *Princ.* 1.2.1; *Comm. John* 1.55.

83. See McDonnell, "Origen," 20, 24. McDonnell calls this a "Logos imperialism" (ibid., 28).

those who remain "worthy," that is, among the sub-set of believers who pursue a life of *ascesis*.[84] Thus, while the thrust of this passage is to demonstrate the eternality of the Spirit, even here we find evidence of potential difficulties.

Indeed, for Origen the eternal existence of the Spirit does not diminish the subordination of the Spirit within the Trinity. Origen is clear that the Father is the "one fount of divinity" (*Princ.* 1.3.7); as Origen spells out elsewhere, the Spirit in fact owes his (uncreated) existence to the Father by the Son.[85] As Henri Crouzel explains, "Only the Father is without origin. The Spirit is then the highest of beings that come from the Father by the Son: that is why He is not called a son."[86] Still, this in no way, Origen takes pains to emphasize, detracts from the fundamental unity of the three *hypostases*; as Origen explains, "nothing in the Trinity can be called greater or less," for "there is no separation in the Trinity" (*Princ.* 1.3.7). All of this, then, helps us understand what form of "subordination" Origen applies to the Spirit (and the Son). On the one hand, the three divine *hypostases* have the *same nature* and are *co-eternal*, and yet there is a distinction with respect to the *manner of their origin*. Thus, it has been argued that Origen's subordinationism could be understood not as ontological but rather as describing the origins of the *hypostases* from eternity past; as Killian McDonnell contends, "subordination in Origen does not rule out identity of nature, or equality in power, or eternity."[87] In later centuries, Origen was charged with a stronger form of subordinationism, as reflected in the critical comments of Jerome and other anti-Origenist writers and would contribute to his condemnation in 553, but scholarship has increasingly recognized that these later controversies reflect more about the people and ideas of those later times than Origen's own thinking.[88] In any event, we will return to the exact nature of Origen's subordinationism below. For now, though, it is worth noting the context that appears to have provoked this particular understanding of

---

84. Heine, *Origen*, 141; McDonnell, "Origen," 21–22; cf. *Princ.* 1.3.7–8, 3.5.8.

85. *Comm. John* 2.10.76; cf. Haykin, *Pneumatomachian Controversy*, 13–15. Widdicombe, *Fatherhood of God*, 74: "All other things, including the Holy Spirit, receive their existence through the mediation of the Son." See also McDonnell, "Origen," 16–18.

86. Crouzel, *Origen*, 201–2. This appears to be the most logical way to reconcile *Comm. John* 2.10.76 with *Princ.* 1.3.3; *contra* Heine, *Origen*, 140. Likewise, later interpolations into *On First Principles* that present a stronger form of subordinationism should not be considered genuine; see further Behr, *Origen: On First Principles*, 1:xxv–xxviii.

87. McDonnell, "Origen," 19.

88. Behr, *Origen: On First Principles*, 1:xxvii.

the Spirit's subordination to the Son. In these passages Origen is arguing specifically against those who were in favor of subordinating the Son to the Spirit, a view which Michel René Barnes terms "hyper-pneumatology."[89] Intriguingly, this view appears to have been popular in Jewish-Christian biblical exegesis, such as that which, like Irenaeus above, identified the Spirit with the Wisdom figure of Prov 8; in summary, Barnes writes, "What Origen accomplishes in his own development of pneumatology is to defeat a Jewish-Christian pneumatology that subordinates Christ by replacing it with a Christology that subordinates the Spirit."[90] Therefore, it is fair to speak of Origen having a "lower" pneumatology than that of Irenaeus, even as Origen continued to advance the understanding of the Spirit in crucially significant ways, as we will now see.

Origen and the Spirit in the Divine Economy

Foundationally, Origen believes in the unity of divine actions among the Trinity, and yet he also maintains that each divine person has his own distinct "operations" or "works" (*proprium*).[91] In the first book of *On First Principles*, the central work of the Spirit is the sanctification of believers.[92] The Spirit does this, in part, through the inspiration of Scripture. As Origen argues, "it is possible in no other way to explain and to bring to human knowledge a higher and more divine teaching regarding the Son than by means of those Scriptures alone which were inspired by the Holy Spirit" (*Princ.* 1.3.1). The Spirit's provision of knowledge concerning the Son thus opens the door to knowledge of the Father; in Origen's words, "all knowledge of the Father is acquired through the revelation of the Son in the Holy Spirit" (*Princ.* 1.3.4). The Spirit thus mediates the Son's knowledge of the Father to believers.[93] It is not surprising, then, when Origen immediately supports this claim with appeal to some of the passages from Scripture that we have seen in this book were central to the early Christian understanding of the Spirit testifying to the Father and the Son (1 Cor 2:10; John 16:12-13, 14:26, 15:26). The implication is that the theme of the Spirit's provision of divine testimony, something that

89. Barnes, "Beginning and End," 182.

90. Barnes, "Beginning and End," 183.

91. McDonnell, "Origen," 19–23.

92. See McDonnell, "Origen," 24; cf. Trigg, *Origen: Bible and Philosophy*, 102–3.

93. See McDonnell, "Origen," 25.

we have traced all the way back to the New Testament itself, continues to exert a significant influence on Origen's pneumatology.

All of this, then, sets the stage for Origen's most important pronouncement concerning the Spirit's revelation of the divine economy in the second book of *On First Principles*. In *Princ.* 2.7, Origen returns to the subject of the Holy Spirit, whom he identifies as the Johannine Paraclete and maintains was the same Spirit who was earlier active in both the prophets and the apostles (*Princ.* 2.7.1). It is only after the ascension of Christ, Origen maintains, that in fulfillment of Joel 2:28 the Spirit has been poured out in such a way that the true (spiritual) meaning of the Old Testament has been unlocked (*Princ.* 2.7.2). This brings Origen to the following conclusion:

> But the Gospel shows [the Spirit] to be of such power and majesty that it says the apostles were not able to receive those things that the Saviour wanted to teach them until the Holy Spirit should come, who, pouring himself into their souls, would be able to enlighten them regarding the nature and faith of the Trinity.[94]

This statement has obvious continuity with what we have seen with Tertullian and other early Christian writers; the Spirit is yet again portrayed as revealing the divine economy to believers. There are, however, two things worthy of special attention in Origen's articulation of this idea. First, Origen explicitly links this work of the Spirit with the Spirit's function of inspiring Scripture. While this idea was of course implicit in earlier writers, Origen develops this idea in far greater detail, in fact devoting almost all of the fourth book of *On First Principles* to detailing his understanding of how to read Scripture in light of this illumination provided by the Spirit, the one who "opens and reveals the sense of spiritual knowledge" (*Princ.* 2.7.4).[95] Second, the Spirit's revelation of the Trinity is explicitly portrayed as having significant ramifications for how to live the Christian life. Tertullian had of course tried, ultimately unsuccessfully, to link the Paraclete's revelation of the divine economy with the discipline of the Paraclete, but here Origen emphasizes the consoling work of the Paraclete to drive a connection between this work of the Spirit and the lived Christian experience. As Origen goes on to explain:

94. *Princ.* 2.7.3.

95. On book 4 of *On First Principles*, see further Behr, *Origen: On First Principles*, 1:xlvi–liv; Dively Lauro, *Soul and Spirit of Scripture*, 37–93.

> For anyone who has deserved to participate in the Holy Spirit, by the knowledge of ineffable mysteries, undoubtedly obtains consolation and gladness of heart. When he has come to know, by the direction of the Spirit, the reasons for all things that happen—why and how they happen—his soul can in no respect be troubled or accept any feeling of sadness; nor is he alarmed by anything, as, clinging to the Word of God and his Wisdom, he calls Jesus "Lord" in the Holy Spirit [1 Cor 12:3].[96]

Thus, the one to whom the Spirit has revealed the "mysteries" of the divine economy is also the one who can persevere through any trial and who can, therefore, call Jesus "Lord" through the Holy Spirit. The quotation of 1 Cor 12:3 again pulls in that key verse as an instance of divine testimony, in which those who "participate in the Holy Spirit" are thereby able to share in his testimony to the lordship of Christ (note, however, the lack of an appeal to prosopological exegesis in making this point, in this regard reflecting Tertullian more than Justin or Irenaeus). Here, then, we have a coming together of the themes of the Spirit's divine testimony and the Spirit's revelation of the divine economy *for the purpose of* instilling faith in believers in the midst of all circumstances. In other words, the Spirit's revelation of the divine economy is not a mere intellectual exercise, nor is it simply to prepare believers for the next life, but it motivates and inspires an entire way of life in the present.[97] Ultimately, this ability of believers to "participate" in the Holy Spirit will have eternal ramifications; as Origen says at the close of *On First Principles*, at the consummation of all things there will be "a diversity of participation in the Father and the Son and the Holy Spirit" (*Princ.* 4.4.9).[98]

In sum, Origen portrays the Spirit as a distinct divine person who reveals the divine economy to believers in order to provide a means of participation in God that begins in this life and is continued in the next. Going beyond Tertullian, Origen identifies the Spirit as eternally present with the Father and the Son. In adopting the language of *hypostasis* rather than *prosōpon* or *persona*, Origen draws more from the well of Platonic philosophy than the realm of prosopological exegesis, and yet the appeals to the Spirit's provision of divine testimony and the Spirit's revelation of the divine economy remain remarkably consistent with the development of those motifs in Irenaeus and Tertullian.

96. *Princ.* 2.7.4.
97. See McDonnell, "Origen," 25.
98. See McDonnell, "Origen," 26.

That being said, Origen's pneumatology still leaves us with some very significant loose ends that would be taken up in the post-Nicene period. Perhaps the most significant concerns the relationship of the Spirit as a *hypostasis* to the other divine *hypostases*. While Tertullian indicated that Father, Son, and Spirit shared one "substance" (*substantia*), Origen never clearly indicates that the Son, much less the Spirit, is of one "essence" (*ousia*) with the Father; the term *homoousios*, so important in later trinitarian reflection, is almost entirely absent in Origen.[99] Second, there remains the problem of Origen's subordinationist language. Even if we read Origen as not himself endorsing an ontological subordinationism, he nevertheless fails to make the case that the Spirit is just as powerful or majestic as the Son.[100] As Joseph Trigg points out, "Since Christ is the link between God and the world in Origen's Platonic system, the Spirit has little obvious place."[101] Perhaps most problematically, he places great distance between the Father on the one hand and the Son and the Spirit on the other; as Origen writes in his *Commentary on John*, in a passage not suspected of interpolation or other forms of textual corruption, "the Father exceeds the Savior as much (or even more) as the Savior himself and the Holy Spirit exceed the rest."[102] There is a sense, then, in which the Spirit is not truly equal with the Father. Likewise, with respect to the economy, the work of the Son is far more expansive than that of the Spirit; as McDonnell concludes, "to deny the Spirit a significant role in creation, to restrict the Spirit's *proprium* because of an imperial Logos is, indeed, a negative factor."[103] Thus, while Origen further solidified the place of the Spirit in the Trinity, the exact nature of the Spirit's place in that Trinity remained somewhat unclear.

Conclusion

In this chapter, we have observed how Irenaeus of Lyons, Tertullian of Carthage, and Origen of Alexandria developed the idea of the Spirit as the

---

99. For further discussion of these issues, see Behr, *Way to Nicaea*, 184–91; McDonnell, "Origen," 15 n. 69. For an argument that Origen did in fact use the term *homoousios*, see Ramelli, "Origen's Anti-Subordinationism," 29–36.

100. McDonnell, "Origen," 34.

101. Trigg, *Origen: Bible and Philosophy*, 102.

102. *Comm. John* 13.151 (trans. Heine); cf. Haykin, *Pneumatomachian Controversy*, 16.

103. McDonnell, "Origen," 30.

one who reveals the divine economy. Again, this comparison has allowed us to trace both continuity and discontinuity. For his part, Irenaeus has extended the earlier theme of the Spirit's provision of divine testimony to the broader notion of the Spirit's revelation of the divine economy, focusing on how the Spirit testifies to the lordship and divinity of the Father and the Son across the entire sweep of salvation history. In so doing, Irenaeus more clearly presents the Spirit as a divine person with a distinct identity and function than had any of his predecessors. Tertullian, meanwhile, built on Irenaeus' understanding of the divine economy to portray the Spirit as revealing that economy to humanity. While Tertullian succeeds in thereby presenting the Spirit as a distinct divine person, part of what he terms the Trinity, his use of a subordinationist theology and his embrace of Montanism would cause serious problems for later theologians. Through our brief examination of how Novatian of Rome constructed his view of the divine economy and the Spirit's place within it (or lack thereof), we demonstrated the likelihood that Tertullian's Montanist leanings led to a diminishment of the person and work of the Holy Spirit among later writers in the Latin West. Therefore, it was to the East, and Origen of Alexandria, that we looked for further elucidation of the Spirit's revelation of the divine economy. For Origen, the Spirit, who along with the Son was eternally generated by the Father, reveals the Trinity to believers; this work of the Spirit, Origen insists, is tightly linked with the Spirit's inspiration of Scripture and strengthening of believers to persevere in faith. Thus, the Spirit's revelation of the divine economy is nothing less than God's means of motivating and inspiring the Christian life. Despite these very significant developments, some of Origen's loose ends concerning whether the Spirit shares in the Father's essence and the nature of the Spirit's subordination would fuel further pneumatological conflict and development in the second half of the fourth century. Still, such was the power of Origen's pneumatology that it is no doubt fair to say, with Anthony Thiselton, that Origen "has developed the doctrine of the Holy Spirit to the point of departure at which Athanasius could take it up in the following century."[104] It is, in fact, with Athanasius that we will begin our next chapter.

Turning back to the mosaic of early Christian pneumatology that is at the heart of this book, we find that the next significant tile helping build the image of the Spirit's unique divine personhood, representing the Spirit's revelation of the divine economy, demonstrates both continuity

104. Thiselton, *Holy Spirit*, 187.

and innovation with the sequence of tiles that has preceded it. While we can see that this tile was again crafted from the raw materials of Scripture, it appears this tile must have come from a slightly different deposit; rather than focusing on particular themes that develop from a close reading of the Old Testament, the emphasis here is instead on how the Spirit provides for a right reading of the Old Testament in light of the Spirit's function of revealing the divine economy. If anything, this tile was set with too much adhesive, representing the continued experience of the Spirit in the Christian community, insofar as Tertullian's embrace of Montanism pushed the exercise of charismata beyond what other tile-layers were willing to allow. To this point, we have focused primarily on the western portion of the mosaic, but with this tile there is something of a pivot, as our gaze now begins to drift towards the eastern section. It is here, in the eastern portion of the mosaic, that we find the final elements that complete the image. The entirety of the mosaic is at last almost in view.

CHAPTER 6

The Spirit and Full Divinity

In the early fourth century, there occurred two events that would have profound ramifications for the future of Christianity. The first was the "conversion" of the emperor Constantine in 312 CE, which would lead to the cessation of persecution against Christians and, ultimately, the dominance of Christianity across Europe. The second was the eruption of the Arian controversy, which was, in some respects, a battle for Origen's legacy. Alexander, the bishop of Alexandria, followed Origen in proclaiming the eternal generation of the Son, while the presbyter Arius laid claim to the legacy of Origen in emphasizing distinctions among the persons of the Trinity and the transcendence of the Father.[1] As the Alexandrian church descended into factional struggle, in 325 Constantine called a council at Nicaea for the purpose of restoring unity. The resulting Nicene Creed, which affirmed that the Son was "begotten not made, consubstantial (*homoousion*) with the Father," hardly put the matter to rest, giving rise to further rounds of acrimonious debates in the following decades.[2] Specifically, opponents of Nicaea maintained that the notion of "order" (*gradus* or *taxis*) within the Godhead required subordination, in the ontological sense, of the Son and the Spirit to the Father; on the other hand, pro-Nicene theologians held to what Lewis Ayres calls "the logic of divine existence as three irreducible agents as sharing or constituting one indivisible divine nature and power."[3]

---

1. Anatolios, *Retrieving Nicaea*, 17; cf. Ayres, *Nicaea and Its Legacy*, 20–30. See also Ramelli, "Origen's Anti-Subordinationism," 24–45; Smith, "Fourth-Century Fathers," 118–20.

2. Anatolios, *Retrieving Nicaea*, 18; cf. Ayres, *Nicaea and Its Legacy*, 85–104.

3. Ayres, "Innovation and *Ressourcement*," 190. For the term "pro-Nicene" theology as "theologies which contain new arguments for or pro Nicaea," see Ayres, *Nicaea and Its Legacy*, 167; cf. ibid., 236–40.

It was in this context that the trinitarian controversy finally became fully trinitarian, for in the second half of the fourth century there emerged a debate among some Christians concerning the nature of the Spirit. Like the debate over the full divinity of the Son, the controversy over the full divinity of the Spirit drew in equal measures from different elements of Origen's teaching. While defenders of the Spirit's coequality with the Father and the Son could draw on Origen's understanding of the Spirit as an eternally existing, distinct *hypostasis*, opponents could appeal to Origen's emphasis on the subordination of the Spirit, identifying the Spirit as part of the Trinity and yet not truly "God."[4]

As we will see, it was during this period that the Spirit would finally be acknowledged as fully divine, a concept that will be unpacked over the course of this chapter. As Ayres summarizes, at this time "the emergence of pro-Nicene trinitarian theologies and their various opponents focused the implicit differences in pneumatology that had been present but largely unexplored in previous decades."[5] In particular, for each of the pro-Nicene writers considered in this chapter—Athanasius, Didymus the Blind, and Basil of Caesarea—we will analyze how their arguments reflected the pneumatological ideas studied thus far in this book. In so doing, we will at last be in position to reflect on the relationship between the Niceno-Constantinopolitan Creed of 381 and the preceding centuries of pneumatological development, allowing us to conclude with a new portrait of the process of the development of the doctrine of the Holy Spirit in the early church.

Athanasius

The first significant pro-Nicene figure whose writings on the Holy Spirit we will examine is Athanasius of Alexandria (ca. 299–373). At the Council of Nicaea, Athanasius served as the principal secretary of his bishop, Alexander, and following Alexander's death in 328 was himself elected bishop of Alexandria.[6] Over the following decades, Athanasius' central role in the Nicene controversy led to him being exiled some five times, even as his writings about Christology and the Trinity would come to be regarded as foundational for later Christian orthodoxy.[7] While the entire scope of Athanasius'

4. See Haykin, *Pneumatomachian Controversy*, 17–18.

5. Ayres, "Innovation and *Ressourcement*," 187.

6. Anatolios, *Athanasius*, 5.

7. On the life of Athanasius, see Anatolios, *Athanasius*, 1–33.

theological vision extends beyond the scope of this book, here we will focus our attention on Athanasius' view of the Holy Spirit.

Athanasius' early writings showed little interest in the doctrine of the Holy Spirit, though in his *Orations against the Arians* he began to move in the direction of affirming the full divinity of the Spirit on the basis of the nature of the Spirit's redemptive work.[8] Athanasius would, however, put forward a more complete and mature articulation of the person and work of the Holy Spirit in the context of the first stage of what is sometimes called the Pneumatomachian controversy, which broke out in the late 350s when a group of Egyptians, of whom we presently know very little, confessed the full divinity of the Son but not of the Spirit.[9] The views of this group were brought to the attention of Athanasius by one of his closest allies, Serapion of Thmuis; according to Athanasius, Serapion reported to him "that certain ones who have withdrawn from the Arians on account of their blasphemy against the Son of God have nonetheless set their minds against the Holy Spirit, claiming not only that he is a creature but also that he is one of *the ministering spirits* [Heb 1:14] and is different from the angels only in degree" (*Ep. Serap.* 1.1.2).[10] Thus, the "Tropikoi," as Athanasius calls his opponents, held to an angelomorphic pneumatology, with appeals to Scripture, both Old and New Testaments, such that the Spirit was created and therefore not fully God.[11] This of course represents a retrieval of earlier such angelomorphic pneumatologies, as had been popular in Alexandrian Christianity, albeit, significantly, now without the emphasis on the Spirit as Creator. By this point, it was well established that the figure of Wisdom in Prov 8 was the Son, and not the Spirit; as we saw earlier in this book, Irenaeus identified Wisdom as the Spirit, but Tertullian and Origen instead applied this passage to the Son.[12] Presumably these Tropikoi were motivated by the concern to preserve the Son's status as the "only-begotten" of the Father, lest the Spirit be conceived of as the Son's brother or even the Son's own son, and therefore they insisted that the Spirit was a creature.[13]

8. See Anatolios, *Athanasius*, 77.

9. See DelCogliano et al., *Works on the Spirit*, 21–22; Haykin, *Pneumatomachian Controversy*, 18–24.

10. All translations of the *Letters to Serapion* are from DelCogliano et al., *Works on the Spirit*.

11. Cf. *Ep. Serap.* 1.3.2, 1.10.4, with reference to Amos 4:13 and 1 Tim 5:21; see further Ayres, "Innovation and *Ressourcement*," 188.

12. For its interpretation in Athanasius' time, see *Ep. Serap.* 1.3.3–4, 2.7.1–3.

13. Cf. *Ep. Serap.* 1.15.1–2; see further Gwynn, *Athanasius*, 90.

With this context in mind, we can now analyze the arguments by which Athanasius asserts the full divinity of the Holy Spirit.

Athanasius and the Full Divinity of the Spirit

In his *Letters to Serapion* (ca. 360), written during his third exile, Athanasius responds to his friend Serapion with arguments against the Tropikoi, drawing on concepts he had earlier developed to prove the full divinity of the Son to likewise demonstrate that the Spirit is not a creature.[14] In the first letter, the longest and most significant, Athanasius first deals with the two biblical texts that his opponents had used to claim that the Spirit was a creature and was counted among the angels, taking pains to distinguish between biblical references to the Holy Spirit and the "spirit" of a human being as well as between biblical references to the Holy Spirit and the angels (*Ep. Serap.* 1.3–14). In the second half of the body of this letter, Athanasius builds his positive case for the full divinity of the Holy Spirit, presenting the Spirit as neither identical with the Son nor one of the creatures, but rather as "proper" to the Son and therefore to the Father, justifying the Spirit's inclusion in the church's trinitarian baptismal formula (*Ep. Serap.* 1.15–31). Throughout, Athanasius consciously extends his reasoning about the Son to his claims about the Spirit; as he puts it in his second letter to Serapion, "For we will find that the way in which we know the Son belongs to the Father corresponds to the way in which the Spirit belongs to the Son" (*Ep. Serap.* 2.10.2). Thus, it was actually Athanasius' participation in debates over Christology that then paved the way for his articulation of his doctrine of the Holy Spirit, even as he drew on pre-existing ideas about the Spirit in order to formulate his arguments, a point that will be explored in more detail below.

At the heart of Athanasius' argument is his conception of the unity of divine agency and action. Thus, the Son "joins us to the Father through the Spirit that is in him" (*Ep. Serap.* 1.24.2). Likewise, "the Father creates and renews all things through the Word in the Holy Spirit" (*Ep. Serap.* 1.24.6). Indeed, "the gifts which the Spirit distributes to each are bestowed by the Father through the Word" (*Ep. Serap.* 1.30.4). In sum, this emerging doctrine of the inseparable operations of the Trinity is described by Athanasius

---

14. For overviews of the *Letters to Serapion*, see Anatolios, *Retrieving Nicaea*, 137–48; Ayres, *Nicaea and Its Legacy*, 211–14; Haykin, *Pneumatomachian Controversy*, 59–67; Thiselton, *Holy Spirit*, 211–13; Weinandy and Keating, *Athanasius*, 29–36.

with the claim that "the Father does all things through the Word in the Holy Spirit" (*Ep. Serap.* 1.28.3). For Athanasius, this identity of activity entails identity of being. As Athanasius explains:

> Seeing that there is such an order and unity in the Holy Trinity, who could separate either the Son from the Father, or the Spirit from the Son or from the Father himself? Who could be so audacious as to say that the Trinity is unlike itself and different in nature? Or that the Son is foreign to the Father in substance? Or that the Spirit is estranged from the Son?[15]

The only logical conclusion, Athanasius insists, is that the Spirit is "proper to the one Word and proper to and the same as the one God in substance (*homoousion*)" (*Ep. Serap.* 1.27.3). At last, Athanasius has asserted that the Spirit is in fact *of one substance* with the Father and the Son. As Khaled Anatolios summarizes, for Athanasius "the Spirit is integral to the organic unity of divine agency, while the inseparability of the activity of Son and Spirit indicates that the Spirit has the same ontological unity with the Son as the Son has with the Father."[16]

In making this claim, Athanasius draws on language he had developed in the christological controversy to speak of the Spirit as "proper to" the Son. By this, Athanasius seems to be drawing on the concept of participation. Echoing earlier such trinitarian analogies, Athanasius appeals to Scripture to show that "the Father is the Fountain and the Son is called the River, and so we are said to drink of the Spirit"; similarly, he suggests, the Father is Light, the Son is Radiance, and the Spirit is the means by which we are enlightened (*Ep. Serap.* 1.19.4). As John Behr writes with respect to Athanasius' understanding of the Son being begotten by the Father, "the Son is, entirely, a participation in the Father's essence; there is no part of the Son that is not always already a participation in the Father."[17] Thus, in the same way, the Spirit participates in the essence of the Son and therefore the essence of the Father, and is not some kind of separation or division from the one divine substance. This emphasis on the unity of the three divine *hypostases* does, however, beg the question of how Athanasius conceives of their distinction. As Anatolios summarizes, "Only the Father is the source; the Son and Spirit are distinguished from one another according to the biblical pattern of imagery, in which the Spirit seems to be the one

15. *Ep. Serap.* 1.20.1.

16. Anatolios, *Athanasius*, 82; cf. Haykin, *Pneumatomachian Controversy*, 76.

17. Behr, *Nicene Faith*, 1:237.

in whom the work of the Son is actualized in humanity."[18] Indeed, as the aforementioned analogies indicated, the special role of the Spirit appears to concern the sanctification and enlightenment of human beings, actions that nevertheless are undertaken in unity with the Son.

On account of this argument, Athanasius has attempted to simultaneously neutralize the problem of the Spirit's subordination by emphasizing the unity of action and identity in the Trinity while also defending the individual identity of the Holy Spirit. As for how exactly these two claims cohere, Athanasius effectively punts the question by appealing to divine mystery (*Ep. Serap.* 1.20.3).[19] Likewise, Athanasius does not aim to distinguish the generation of the Son from that of the Spirit or otherwise explain how the Spirit is distinguished within the divine being itself.[20] Perhaps the closest that Athanasius comes to addressing these questions is his claim that "as the Son is in the Spirit as in his own Image, so too is the Father in the Son" (*Ep. Serap.* 1.20.4). As Thomas Weinandy and Daniel Keating write, "The notion of a progressive 'imaging' does allow Athanasius to maintain the divine triadic unity as well as the distinct identity of the Father, the Son, and the Holy Spirit, for the Son is the begotten image of the Father and the Holy Spirit proceeds as the image of the Son," and yet there is a problem insofar as "the Holy Spirit does not perfectly reflect the Son's sonship as the Son perfectly reflects the Father's fatherhood."[21] Likewise problematic was Athanasius' presentation of the Spirit as the "activity" or "energy" (*energeia*) of the Son, which threatened to undermine the reality of the Spirit's real and distinct divine subsistence.[22] Issues related to this particular wording will be taken up by Didymus and especially by Basil, as we will see below. Still, as Anatolios argues, "Athanasius nevertheless has all the component features" of what would come to be orthodox trinitarian theology, asserting "that both the real unity and real distinction are integral to the Christian identification of God."[23]

One other aspect of Athanasius' argument for the full divinity of the Holy Spirit is worth our brief attention. Perhaps sensing that his appeals to Scripture, which dominate the entirety of the preceding sections of the

18. Anatolios, *Athanasius*, 83.

19. See further Weinandy and Keating, *Athanasius*, 30.

20. See Anatolios, *Retrieving Nicaea*, 25, 143.

21. Weinandy and Keating, *Athanasius*, 31.

22. Cf. *Ep. Serap.* 1.20.5; see further Ayres, *Nicaea and Its Legacy*, 214.

23. Anatolios, *Retrieving Nicaea*, 145.

letter, were not fully persuasive, Athanasius concludes with one final line of argument, from the tradition of the church: "In addition to these arguments, let us also examine the tradition, teaching, and faith of the Catholic Church from the beginning" (*Ep. Serap.* 1.28.1).[24] Athanasius' central claim is that, following Matt 28:19, the one baptism is performed in the name of the Father, and of the Son, and of the Holy Spirit; by rendering the Spirit a creature, the Tropikoi have divided the Trinity and rendered baptism invalid.[25] This, then, appears to be what Athanasius is referring to when he speaks of the "one faith in the Trinity handed down to us" (*Ep. Serap.* 1.30.1). The historical significance of this appeal to tradition is that, on the one hand, it looks back to earlier seeds of such ideas, as in Origen, while it also anticipates further development, especially from Basil of Caesarea, whom we will examine below.[26] Theologically, Athanasius thus linked the Spirit's presence at baptism with the Spirit's role in sanctifying and divinizing believers insofar as baptism "initiates into the Trinity" (*Ep. Serap.* 1.30.1). The divinity of the Holy Spirit is essential to this process, he argues, because "the one in whom creatures are divinized cannot himself be external to the divinity of the Father" (*Ep. Serap.* 1.25.5). In baptism, therefore, believers participate in the Spirit, who participates in the Son, who in turn participates in the Father; thus, Christians partake in God's own life.[27] This too, we will see, plays a role in Basil's subsequent argumentation.

In sum, Athanasius has appealed to Scripture and tradition to demonstrate that the Spirit is fully divine, appealing especially to the inseparable operations of the Trinity that demonstrate the unity of divine substance.[28] Unlike Origen, Athanasius explicitly asserts that the Spirit is *homoousios* with the Father and the Son, and he makes no suggestion that the Spirit is any way less in authority, glory, or significance than the Father

---

24. See Haykin, *Pneumatomachian Controversy*, 93–94; Gwynn, *Athanasius*, 91; Weinandy and Keating, *Athanasius*, 34–35.

25. See *Ep. Serap.* 1.28.4, 1.29.2–3. Arguments over the implications of the baptismal formula for the Christian understanding of God were in fact common in the fourth century; see further Anatolios, *Retrieving Nicaea*, 145–46.

26. For Origen's comments on the Spirit's place in the baptismal formula, see *Princ.* 1.3.2.

27. See Smith, "Fourth-Century Fathers," 121.

28. Interestingly, despite making this strong case for the Spirit's full divinity, Athanasius, like Basil of Caesarea after him, nevertheless does not explicitly call the Spirit "God," perhaps in light of the fact that Scripture does not ever directly say this; cf. Weinandy and Keating, *Athanasius*, 29 n. 10.

or the Son. The problem for Athanasius seems to be that his account of how the three divine *hypostases* are therefore distinguished appears somewhat underdeveloped.

Athanasius and Pre-Nicene Pneumatology

At this point, we can now analyze Athanasius' relationship to the four pivotal pneumatological themes we have traced from the pre-Nicene period. As a result, we will be able to see that there is more continuity between Athanasius and his predecessors than is usually acknowledged in traditional accounts of the development of early Christian views of the Spirit, which tend to marginalize developments in the pre-Nicene period, as well as to note some of the innovative ways in which Athanasius extends and further develops earlier pneumatological ideas.

First, with respect to the Spirit's provision of divine testimony, Athanasius makes extensive use of the key passages referenced in chapter 2 of this book. Athanasius makes frequent reference to the Spirit as the Paraclete, twice quoting John 15:26 to identify the Spirit as the "Spirit of Truth."[29] What Athanasius does with this text in light of his interest in the inseparable activity of Son and Spirit is quite interesting. As argued earlier in this book, in the Johannine context the truth that the Spirit leads believers into is the proper understanding of Jesus' person and work, a task that the Spirit is uniquely equipped to perform because of the Spirit's intimate union with Jesus, who had himself stated, "I am . . . the truth" (John 14:6). Athanasius picks up on this connection, pulling in Jesus' statement to the Samaritan woman about true worshippers worshiping the Father in Spirit and truth (John 4:21–24) to conclude that "true worshippers worship the Father but in Spirit and Truth, confessing the Son and the Spirit who is in him" (*Ep. Serap.* 1.33.4). Athanasius then reverses the direction of the motif of divine testimony to show how Christ himself "bears witness" to the inseparability of Father, Son, and Spirit, thereby demonstrating that the Spirit is truly God (*Ep. Serap.* 1.33.4). Thus, not only does the Spirit testify in truth to the divinity of the Son, but *the Son testifies in truth to the divinity of the Spirit*. This extension of the theme of divine testimony shows continuity both with earlier exegesis about the Spirit and divine testimony and with Athanasius' ideas about divine unity and the

29. For citations of John 15:26, see *Ep. Serap.* 1.11.6, 1.25.3–4; for quotations of other Paraclete passages, see also *Ep. Serap.* 1.4.1, 1.6.2, 1.11.1, 1.20.6–7. Athanasius also cites and interprets 1 Cor 2:10–12 at *Ep. Serap.* 1.22.1.

full divinity of the Holy Spirit. Indeed, for Athanasius the testimony of the Spirit *is* the testimony of the Son.[30]

Second, concerning the Spirit and Christian identity, Athanasius simply assumes the unity of the Testaments' testimony to the Holy Spirit. Because "the Holy Spirit is recognized in all the Divine Scriptures" (*Ep. Serap.* 1.7.1), Athanasius can make use of evidence from both Old and New Testaments as speaking of one Holy Spirit.[31] To recall our discussion in chapter 3 about how the author of the Epistle of Barnabas identified many of the most famous Old Testament figures as looking forward to Christ in the Spirit, we find Athanasius making a similar exegetical move. Moses, Athanasius argues, was not simply a Christian, he was in fact a pro-Nicene theologian, for Moses not only "knows that the angels are creatures, but that the Holy Spirit is united to the Son and the Father" (*Ep. Serap.* 1.12.1). Again, we have evidence of Athanasius articulating pneumatological ideas that clearly echo earlier arguments concerning the person and work of the Spirit even as they are "updated" for his own context and his need to prove that the Spirit is not simply a key element of Christian identity but is in fact fully divine.

Third, on the theme of how person-language is applied to the Spirit, Athanasius continues to make use of the reading strategy of prosopological exegesis. In particular, he notes that even his opponents correctly identify the true speaker of Prov 8:22 as the Word; it cannot be the Spirit, he insists, because there is no contextual clue that the Holy Spirit is in view (*Ep. Serap.* 1.3.3–4). Indeed, Athanasius is following a tradition that rejected Irenaeus' identification of Wisdom as the Spirit and instead applied this passage to the person of the Son. Intriguingly, however, Athanasius retrieves some notion of the Spirit as Creator when he asserts that all things "have their strength to exist through the Spirit" (*Ep. Serap.* 2.14.1), a theme that is then picked up by the Cappadocians.[32] Still, it is striking that arguments from prosopological exegesis from the person of the Holy Spirit have fallen away entirely at this point; Athanasius even cites and prosopologically interprets the words of Ps 45:6–7 as being spoken to the Son, but presents the speaker simply as David and not as the Holy Spirit, as Justin and Irenaeus had (*Ep. Serap.* 2.4.5, 2.8.2).

---

30. See *Ep. Serap.* 1.31.9–12.

31. See *Ep. Serap.* 1.7.3–6.

32. See Ayres, "Innovation and *Ressourcement*," 194; DelCogliano et al., *Works on the Spirit*, 25.

Finally, considering the theme of the Spirit's revelation of the divine economy, we find that Athanasius is also, in his disputes with the Arians and the Tropikoi, engaged in mapping or ordering the spirit world. The issue concerning the Holy Spirit, then, is whether the Spirit should be "classified with the angels" on account of the Spirit belonging "to their order" (*Ep. Serap.* 1.10.4). Athanasius in fact connects this attempt to order the spiritual realm with the heretical ideas of Valentinus, and insists that making the Spirit one of the angels would have the effect of making all the angels part of the Trinity (*Ep. Serap.* 1.10.5). Though there is nevertheless "order" in the Trinity, there is a still a fundamental "unity" among Father, Son, and Spirit (*Ep. Serap.* 1.20.1), as described above. Within the Trinity, the Spirit "sanctifies and enlightens" (*Ep. Serap.* 1.20.5), actions that are fundamentally participatory; "it is through the Spirit that all of us are said to be partakers of God" (*Ep. Serap.* 1.24.1). The Spirit, then, is the one who "divinizes" (*Ep. Serap.* 1.24.4). This emphasis on revelation, participation, and divinization of course recalls Origen's understanding of the Holy Spirit, demonstrating yet another continuity with pre-Nicene pneumatology.

In sum, Athanasius both advances the doctrine of the Holy Spirit forward by moving beyond a subordinationist account of the Spirit's place in the Trinity, even as he demonstrates clear indebtedness to the ideas of many of the pre-Nicene writers examined earlier in this book. Throughout, the significance of the Old Testament for this theological process and the importance of the Spirit for the Christian life continued to be assumed, just as they were in prior centuries.

Didymus the Blind

Didymus the Blind (ca. 313–398), a contemporary and ally of Athanasius in Alexandria, was a renowned teacher and biblical exegete despite having been blinded at an early age and not having received an advanced education.[33] Probably written shortly after Athanasius' *Letters to Serapion*, Didymus' short treatise *On the Holy Spirit* (ca. 365) has many similarities with those letters of Athanasius, suggesting that Didymus was aware of them even as he drew on additional sources in composing his own work.[34]

---

33. On Didymus' life and education, see Layton, *Didymus the Blind*, 13–26; DelCogliano et al., *Works on the Spirit*, 31–36.

34. See DelCogliano et al., *Works on the Spirit*, 37–42, 46–47.

In *On the Holy Spirit*, Didymus appears to be responding to ideas similar to those that called forth Athanasius' *Letters to Serapion*, seeking to provide his students with scriptural support for the full deity of the Spirit against the claims of some that the Spirit was a created being who should be counted among the angels.[35] Didymus may have also been responding to the claims of Eunomius of Cyzicus, who had suggested in his *Apology* (ca. 360) that because the Father alone is ungenerated, the Father alone is truly God, and therefore the Son and the Holy Spirit cannot be *homoousios* with the Father.[36] Regardless of the exact relationship of Didymus' opponents to those of Athanasius, we can now examine how Didymus makes his case for the full divinity of the Holy Spirit.

Didymus and the Full Divinity of the Spirit

Given the myriad similarities between the writings of Athanasius and Didymus on the Holy Spirit, a brief summary of Didymus' major points will suffice. Like Athanasius, Didymus asserts the inseparability of Father, Son, and Spirit, demonstrating from Scripture their common activity, which for him necessitates that they share a single substance.[37] Didymus, however, pursues this line of argumentation in more detail, thereby providing a firmer foundation for distinguishing the Son and the Spirit. For it is the case, Didymus suggests, that even in this common activity each of the divine *hypostases* has its own particular mission in the world. Didymus unpacks this idea with respect to the Spirit as it concerns the Spirit's work of sanctification.

On the one hand, all three *hypostases* share in the work of sanctification, as holiness is part of the shared divine nature, and so Didymus can also speak of the Son as one who sanctifies (*Spir.* 17). And yet there is also a sense in which the Holy Spirit has a special mission with respect to sanctification, for the Spirit sanctifies believers "by the bestowal of himself" (*Spir.* 26).[38] This point about believers being sanctified as they participate in the Spirit is of enormous importance for Didymus, for if the Spirit is

35. See *Spir.* 1–2; DelCogliano et al., *Works on the Spirit*, 43–44.

36. DelCogliano et al., *Works on the Spirit*, 40; on Eunomius, see further Smith, "Fourth-Century Fathers," 114–15; Behr, *Nicene Faith*, 2:271–82.

37. See, e.g., *Spir.* 81, 86, 145, 161.

38. Cf. *Spir.* 11–20, 24–29. All translations of Didymus' *On the Holy Spirit* are from DelCogliano et al., *Works on the Spirit*.

capable of being participated in and is not himself one who participates in another, his substance is immutable and he is not a creature but rather of one substance with the Father and the Son.[39] This has implications, for instance, in how we understand the Spirit to function as the "Spirit of Wisdom" or the "Spirit of Truth":

> Therefore, since the Spirit of Wisdom and Truth is inseparable from the Son, he too is Wisdom and Truth. If he were to participate in wisdom and truth, at some point he could descend into a state of ceasing to possess what he received from somewhere, namely, wisdom and truth. And the Son, who is himself Wisdom and Truth, is not separated from the Father, whom the words of the Scriptures proclaim as the *Only-Wise* [Rom 16:27] and Truth. We will see that the Holy Spirit, because he is the Spirit of Wisdom and Truth, possesses the same circle of unity and substance as the Son, and, moreover, that the Son is not divided from the substance of the Father.[40]

The Spirit, then, like the Father and the Son, himself subsists as Wisdom and Truth.[41] The only logical conclusion for Didymus, then, is that "the Trinity is of one substance" (*Spir.* 76). In this way Didymus provides an account of the Holy Spirit that demonstrates both the unity of the *hypostases* with regards to their common substance and activity, while also showing their distinction with respect to the particularity of their missions.[42]

Like Athanasius, Didymus makes an appeal to the tradition of the church, likewise pointing to the trinitarian baptismal formula as evidence of the indivisibility of the Trinity (*Spir.* 99–103). Interestingly, however, Didymus extends this line of argument further, next taking up the subject of the Spirit's role in church discipline, demonstrating that the Spirit, like the Father and the Son, establishes the leaders of the church (*Spir.* 104–105). We also discover in Didymus concern with the language of the Holy

---

39. See *Spir.* 16–19, 24–29, 54–56; DelCogliano et al., *Works on the Spirit*, 45–46. Athanasius began to develop similar ideas at *Ep. Serap.* 1.23.1–3, 1.27.1–2. On the notion of the Spirit as the "undiminished giver," see further Ayres, "Holy Spirit as 'Undiminished Giver,'" 58–59.

40. *Spir.* 94.

41. DelCogliano et al., *Works on the Spirit*, 47; Ayres, "Holy Spirit as 'Undiminished Giver,'" 70–72.

42. Didymus develops this idea in more detail and with more precision in a treatise, *On the Trinity*, that should in all likelihood be ascribed to him; see further Hicks, *Trinity, Economy, and Scripture*, 89–107.

Spirit as an "activity" or "energy" (*energeia*) of God; with reference to the gifts of the Spirit in 1 Cor 12, Didymus explains that "the nature of [the] Holy Spirit is active and 'distributing,'" and so urges us to "not be taken in by those who say that the Holy Spirit is an activity and not the substance of God" (*Spir.* 97).[43] Didymus' precision on this point thus places him closer to the conception of Basil of Caesarea than his contemporary Athanasius. Not surprisingly, then, Didymus can be quite explicit in his assertion that the Spirit is God.[44] Further differences between Didymus' account of the Holy Spirit and that of Athanasius will be taken up as we examine the extent to which Didymus' writings echo the key pneumatological themes of pre-Nicene writers, a topic to which we now turn.

Didymus and Pre-Nicene Pneumatology

Following the procedure established above with Athanasius, we will now consider the extent to which Didymus' writings demonstrate continuity with the four key pneumatological themes from the pre-Nicene period that we have analyzed earlier in this book. Given the overlap in time, geography, and content between Didymus' and Athanasius' writings on the Spirit, direct comparison between these two can further illuminate our study of this topic.

First, on the subject of the Spirit's provision of divine testimony, we find that Didymus follows Athanasius and his pre-Nicene predecessors by utilizing the Johannine Paraclete passages and identifying the Holy Spirit as the Spirit of Truth. Comparatively speaking, though, the great extent to which Didymus reflects on these ideas in detail is striking. In the first such lengthy passage, Didymus unpacks the nature of the Spirit's procession and sending (*Spir.* 110–124). Quoting John 15:26, Didymus acknowledges the Spirit's role in providing testimony to the Son, which he then links to the Father's testimony to the Son, thereby continuing his overall focus on the inseparable operations of the divine persons (*Spir.* 116). What is also interesting about Didymus' use of this verse is how extensively he utilizes a different part of the verse to make an argument about the nature of the Spirit's procession from the Father and to note that the Spirit is sent by both

---

43. Cf. *Spir.* 76; cp. *Ep. Serap.* 1.20.5. See further Radde-Gallwitz, "Holy Spirit," 236–41. On similar concerns in Basil of Caesarea, see Ayres, *Nicaea and Its Legacy*, 215–16.

44. See, e.g., *Spir.* 83, 130, 224.

the Father and the Son.[45] Given the importance of this verse in establishing the theme of the Spirit's divine testimony to the Son and the notion of the Spirit's personhood, it is perhaps fitting that this verse is again the locus of further reflection on the Spirit's place in the Trinity. The second and even longer major section dealing with the Johannine Paraclete passages consists of extended commentary on John 14:26 and John 16:12–15 (*Spir.* 132–174). Concerning the former, Didymus again appeals to the notion of inseparable operations to show that the teaching work of the Holy Spirit is in fact the same as the teaching ministry of the Father and the Son. Emphasizing that the Spirit is not one who has learned from another teacher but is in fact himself the Spirit of Truth, Didymus writes that "he invisibly imparts knowledge of divine things to the mind" (*Spir.* 141). Thus, Didymus not only connects John 14:26 to another significant pre-Nicene theme, that of the Spirit's revelation of the divine economy, but he also again (as with John 15:26) interprets this verse in such a way as to further support his doctrine of inseparable operations and thereby defend the full divinity of the Holy Spirit. Finally, as for John 16:12–15, Didymus argues that the truth into which the Paraclete will lead believers results in moving them "from the death of the letter to the Spirit that gives life," for "in him alone resides all the truth of Scripture" (*Spir.* 150). Given that the Son is in fact himself "Truth," when Didymus suggests that "God grants this perfection by sending the Spirit of Truth who guides believers into the whole Truth," the implication is that this knowledge is participatory, uniting believers with Christ (*Spir.* 152). The Spirit, therefore, does not simply provide testimony by teaching some abstract form of knowledge of the deity and lordship of Christ, but rather *makes this knowledge an enacted reality.* In joining the themes of divine testimony and participation in Christ, Didymus crafts a complex and creative approach to the doctrine of the Holy Spirit.

Second, concerning earlier battles over the Spirit between Jews and Christians, Didymus parallels Athanasius in simply assuming the unity of the Testaments' testimony to the Holy Spirit. As Didymus says near the start of his work, "no one ought to consider that the Holy Spirit was one thing in the saints before the coming of the Lord and another thing in the Apostles and the other disciples, as if the same name indicated different realities" (*Spir.* 6).[46] As such, Didymus draws on both the Old and New Testaments

---

45. See *Spir.* 114, 117, 120.

46. Cf. *Spir.* 197, 203–205.

to demonstrate the full divinity of the Holy Spirit.[47] Didymus also further develops the Christian understanding of the Spirit ceasing from Judaism. In his discussion of Isa 63:10, Didymus applies the idea that those who did not believe "enraged the Holy Spirit" against the Jews, who crucified Christ. The result of this was that the Jews "were handed over to the Romans when the wrath of God came upon them in the end," and now "wander alone in foreign lands as exiles from their homeland, having neither their ancient city nor their own habitations" (*Spir.* 215–216). This unfortunate (and ultimately not necessary notion for the development of the doctrine of the Holy Spirit as a distinct divine person) anti-Semitism is indeed a further development of earlier ideas about the Spirit and Christian identity; not only did the Spirit abandon the Jews for the Christians, but the Spirit is actively engaged in punishing the Jews in these various ways. In other words, in linking the Spirit and Christian identity, Didymus is also linking the Spirit and anti-Semitism, at least as we would understand that today.

Third, on the topic of person-language as applied to the Spirit, Didymus' close reading of Scripture and his concern to correctly identify the speakers and audience of different quotations leads him to occasional use of prosopological exegesis as we have defined it, albeit without explicit invocation of terms such as *prosōpon*.[48] For our purposes, one significant move that Didymus makes in this regard again concerns his doctrines of inseparable operations and identity of substance. Didymus notes that while Paul, in Acts 28:25–26, attributes the words spoken to the prophet Isaiah in Isa 6:8–11 as being the words of the Holy Spirit, the text of the Isaiah passage clearly indicates that these were the words of the Lord, Christ (*Spir.* 128–129). Rather than distinguish between the Spirit speaking as a primary speaking agent and as an inspiring secondary agent, Didymus instead uses this as evidence that "the Lord and the Holy Spirit have the same will and nature, and that the name of the Lord is also to be understood when the Spirit is mentioned" (*Spir.* 130). Intriguingly, whereas prosopological exegesis was used in the pre-Nicene period to *distinguish* between the divine persons, Didymus appeals to the identities of speakers of biblical quotations to demonstrate the *unity* of these divine persons. A second item of interest is found in Didymus' extended discussion of divine speech, in which he insists

---

47. See, e.g., *Spir.* 7–8, 125–129, 197–230.

48. See, e.g., *Spir.* 7, 51, 228. The one use of "person" (*prosōpon*) with reference to the Trinity is in *Spir.* 133, apart from any discussion of divine speech; cf. DelCogliano et al., *Works on the Spirit*, 185 n. 107.

that with respect to all biblical reports of dialogue among divine persons, "we should not understand this as taking place in the manner to which we are accustomed when we converse and speak among ourselves in turn, but in the way that conforms with incorporeal natures" (*Spir.* 154). Here we are reminded of the *metaphorical* nature of the personhood that is envisioned in these divine conversations, something that was perhaps implicit in pre-Nicene authors but is made explicit here. For Didymus, this is yet another excuse to point back to the inseparable actions and unity of substance of the Trinity, further demonstrating his adaptation of pre-Nicene ideas in service of his pro-Nicene agenda (*Spir.* 158–159).

Lastly, on the subject of how the Spirit reveals the divine economy, Didymus posits that the Spirit teaches "the mysteries of truth and wisdom," the "knowledge of divine things" (*Spir.* 140–141). This work of the Spirit appears to be part of his broader function of cleansing or renewing the mind, and the content of this knowledge, as the context of the treatise would indicate, concerns proper knowledge of the Trinity.[49] Typical is Didymus' conclusion that "when the Spirit of Truth himself enters into a pure and simple mind, he will impress upon you the knowledge of truth; since he always joins the new to the old, he will guide you into all truth" (*Spir.* 151). Didymus thus appears to suggest that having an undisturbed mind is a prerequisite for receiving the fullness of the Holy Spirit, although he does not elaborate on what precisely he means by this. Where he does develop the notion of the Spirit's work in revealing the divine economy is, unsurprisingly by this point, in the context of his affirmation of the inseparable operations of the Trinity. For Didymus, not only does the Spirit reveal the Son, who in turn reveals the Father, but it is also the case that the Father reveals the Son, who in turn reveals the Spirit "by bestowing him on those who have prepared themselves to be worthy of his gift and by distributing to them the sublimity of his glorification and greatness" (*Spir.* 169). The revelation of the divine economy is, therefore, an action of the entire Trinity.

Across each of these four key pre-Nicene pneumatological themes, it is striking how Didymus has adapted each of them in the service of his argument for inseparable operations and therefore unity of substance among Father, Son, and Holy Spirit, which leads to the inescapable conclusion that the Spirit is indeed fully and truly God. In this way, Didymus has both drawn on and updated for his own polemical concerns each of these significant points.

49. See *Spir.* 10, 44, 142–143, 149.

Basil of Caesarea

With Basil of Caesarea (ca. 330–379), we arrive at a figure characterized by "a life-long preoccupation with the subject and person of the Holy Spirit."[50] Writing more than a decade after the aforementioned works of Athanasius and Didymus, Basil engaged in a later stage of the controversy over the full deity of the Holy Spirit.[51] As bishop of Caesarea, Basil came into conflict with his old friend and mentor Eustathius, in large part over the doctrine of the Holy Spirit. To simplify a very complex story, Eustathius had come to lead a group sometimes termed the "Macedonians" or "Pneumatoma-chians" (that is, the "Spirit-fighters"), who denied the divinity of the Holy Spirit but not of the Son.[52] Their stumbling block in affirming the Spirit's full divinity appears to have been the lack of explicit scriptural support for the notion.[53] Rather, they insisted, the Spirit "must not be ranked with the Father and the Son, because he is different in nature and lacking in dignity" (*Spir.* 10.24).[54] Unlike Athanasius' opponents, this group seems to have constituted what Lewis Ayres calls "a distinct sect with a very limited alternative hierarchy."[55]

It was in the face of this powerful and well-organized opposition, then, that Basil penned his treatise *On the Holy Spirit* (ca. 375), written to his protégé Amphilochius, the bishop of Iconium.[56] Scholars have suggested that much of the treatise is in fact drawn from a transcription of Basil's confrontation with Eustathius at Sebaste, which likely took place in June of 373.[57] In any event, it is to this work, and its arguments for the full divinity of the Holy Spirit, to which we now turn.

---

50. Haykin, *Pneumatomachian Controversy*, 104. On Basil's life and significance, see Behr, *Nicene Faith*, 2:263–67; Hildebrand, *Trinitarian Theology*, 18–29.

51. Didymus appears to have been a particularly noteworthy source for Basil; see DelCogliano, "Basil of Caesarea, Didymus the Blind," 656–58.

52. On the complex theological disagreements, church politics, and shifting alliances surrounding the writing of *On the Holy Spirit*, see Haykin, *Pneumatomachian Controversy*, 24–49; Hildebrand, *Basil of Caesarea*, 71–80.

53. Hildebrand, *Basil of Caesarea*, 78.

54. Cf. Haykin, *Pneumatomachian Controversy*, 120. All translations of Basil's *On the Holy Spirit* are from Hildebrand, *On the Holy Spirit*.

55. Ayres, *Nicaea and Its Legacy*, 215.

56. For an overview of *On the Holy Spirit*, see Haykin, *Pneumatomachian Controversy*, 105–13.

57. Haykin, *Pneumatomachian Controversy*, 108–13.

Basil and the Full Divinity of the Spirit

As we have seen with Athanasius and Didymus, Basil draws on arguments used to prove the full divinity of the Son, emphasizing the unity of divine action and nature, to now demonstrate the full divinity of the Spirit. Basil affirms that "in everything the Holy Spirit is indivisible and inseparable from the Father and the Son" (*Spir.* 16.37). Within this notion of inseparable operations, Basil elaborates on how a single work of God contains elements of creating, redeeming, and perfecting. As Lewis Ayres explains, "Basil presents the peculiar action of the Spirit, completing and sanctifying, as a constant part or aspect of God's activity."[58] Basil is much less interested than his predecessors, though, in going on to unpack the technical language to explain this view of God. The result is that Basil succeeds in affirming the inseparable operations of the Trinity while carving out a clear and distinct role for the Spirit in the economy of salvation, even as he continues to neglect the question of the Spirit's position relative to the Father and the Son prior to creation.[59] Rather, Basil moves to the front and center of his argument something that was present, albeit seemingly less significant, in the writings of his predecessors: the theological implications of the role of the Spirit in baptism and the church's liturgy.

Basil's concern for how the church's worship should contribute to the church's understanding of the Holy Spirit is a major theme throughout the treatise. In fact, the very opening of the treatise indicates it was written in part to address a liturgical concern over the trinitarian formula for rendering glory to God, as Basil defends his usage of both "to the Father, with the Son together with the Holy Spirit, and to the Father, through the Son, in the Holy Spirit," leading into an extended discussion of prepositions as applied to the divine persons (*Spir.* 1.3).[60] Having then undertaken an extensive discussion of the use of prepositions with respect to the divine persons (*Spir.* 2.4—8.21),[61] Basil at the outset of the central portion of the treatise first responds to the charge that the Holy Spirit should not rank with the Father and the Son by pointing to the trinitarian baptismal formula. Citing Matt 28:19, he argues, "if the Lord had not joined the Spirit to himself and to the

58. Ayres, *Nicaea and Its Legacy*, 216, with reference to *Spir.* 16.37–40.

59. See Ayres, *Nicaea and Its Legacy*, 217.

60. Haykin, *Pneumatomachian Controversy*, 106: "This doxological question is more than simply the immediate occasion for the composition of *Spir.* As a major pattern in the tapestry of the treatise, it provides the treatise with coherence."

61. This topic is then revisited at *Spir.* 25.58—29.75.

Father in baptism, then let them not blame us for the joining, for we neither think nor say anything different" (*Spir.* 10.24). Here Basil explicitly refutes those who demand more explicit scriptural proof for his position, instead appealing to "the non-scriptural witness of the fathers" (*Spir.* 10.25). Indeed, for Basil the preeminent argument for the Spirit's full divinity is the content of the confession made at baptism:

> On account of what are we Christians? Everyone would say, "On account of faith." How are we saved? Clearly we are regenerated through the grace of baptism. How else? So then knowing that this salvation is established through the Father, and the Son, and the Holy Spirit, should we cast away the *standard of teaching* [Rom 6:17] which we have received? . . . Am I to be turned aside by their arguments of plausibility and to surrender the tradition that leads me to the light and that has graced me with the knowledge of God, through which I have been received as a child of God, I who up until this time was an enemy because of my sin? Rather, I pray that I depart to the Lord with this confession, and I urge them to keep the faith free from violence until the day of Christ and to guard the Spirit undivided from the Father and the Son. Thus they will closely observe the teaching received at baptism both in their confession of faith and in rendering glory.[62]

In this remarkable passage, Basil is basically articulating the notion of *lex orandi, lex credendi*: "the rule of prayer is the rule of belief."[63] It is liturgy, rooted in the apostolic tradition of the church, that ultimately shapes theology, and not what he dismisses as "arguments of plausibility." Khaled Anatolios terms this a "sacramental epistemology," which is fundamentally concerned "to insist on a chain of continuity between knowledge of God, participation in divine life, and the material form of the sacramental event that initiates and actualizes that participation (i.e., the baptismal formula of the triune name)."[64] While gestures in this direction were made in earlier writers, Basil develops and utilizes this idea to a far greater extent. The result is not simply a defense of the doctrine of the full divinity of the Holy Spirit, but in fact the articulation of a more nuanced theological method. As Michael Haykin summarizes, "Despite the fact that Scripture was not replete

---

62. *Spir.* 10.26.

63. Cf. *Spir.* 27.67: "according to the logic of piety, as we baptize, so we ought to believe."

64. Anatolios, *Retrieving Nicaea*, 208. On Basil's soteriology, and its relationship to his understanding of baptism, see further Hildebrand, *Trinitarian Theology*, 173–78.

with evidence for the Spirit's divinity, the faithful exegete would shape his exegesis according to the testimony of those Scriptures which were most explicit about the Spirit, of which the chief was Mt 28:19, and according to the experience and tradition of the church."[65] Scriptural exegesis was still the cornerstone of the development of doctrine, and yet the liturgy of the church "provided keys that unlocked the depths of Scriptural passages."[66] Scripture and tradition, for Basil, are therefore not so much two distinct sources for theology as they are one interrelated whole.[67]

Finally, Basil's case for the full divinity of the Holy Spirit advances the notions of divine transcendence and simplicity.[68] In presenting Father, Son, and Spirit as coequal members of the triune God, Basil argues that "it is best to let what is unattainable remain beyond number," and yet "if, however, you must count, at least do not harm the truth in so doing" (*Spir.* 18.44). As Didymus reminded us that the personhood envisioned in divine dialogues recorded in Scripture is metaphorical in nature, Basil pushes us to see how, in light of God's transcendence, even the notion of God as three persons (in his terminology, *hypostases*) is a concession to a reality that human words can only approximate. And yet, Basil insists, if we proclaim three distinct persons, this must not imply polytheism; rather, the divine nature is simple, for there is one "common nature" and therefore "one thing" (*Spir.* 18.45). How does Basil reconcile this? Here he addresses the challenge head-on and offers an analogy:

> How, then, if [the Father and the Son] are one and one, are there not two gods? Because it is said that there is a king and the image of a king, but not two kings, for the power is not divided, and the glory is not portioned out. As the power that rules over us and the authority is one, so also one, not many, is the doxology from us. On account of this, the honor of the image passes over to the archetype. Therefore, the image is the prototype by way of imitation [in the case of the king and his image]; the Son is this by nature. And just as in the arts there is a likeness according to

65. Haykin, *Pneumatomachian Controversy*, 117.

66. Haykin, *Pneumatomachian Controversy*, 116.

67. That being said, Basil does approve of certain Christian liturgical formulas or practices on the basis of tradition entirely apart from any explicit scriptural source; cf. *Spir.* 27.66. For the difference between "dogmas" and "proclamations" in Basil's thought, see further Hildebrand, *Basil of Caesarea*, 92–96; Hildebrand, *Trinitarian Testimony*, 141–49.

68. This discussion follows that of Hildebrand, *On the Holy Spirit*, 23–25.

form, so with the divine and incomposite nature, the unity is in the communion of the Godhead.[69]

Basil takes up this same language of the divine "image" and explicitly extends it to the Spirit later in the treatise, where he contends that "just as we speak of worship in the Son as worship in the Image of God the Father, so also we speak of worship in the Spirit as worship in him who manifests the divinity of the Lord," for "it is impossible to see the Image of the invisible God, except in the illumination of the Spirit" (*Spir.* 26.64). Thus, the unity of Father, Son, and Spirit in the baptismal formula reflects the ontological unity of Father, Son, and Spirit, who together bring about the salvation of human beings.[70] The idea, then, is that the archetype (the Father) is inseparable from its image (the Son) and the light in which that image is revealed (the Spirit).[71] In continuing this image, Basil pulls in one of his favorite Pauline texts on the Holy Spirit:

> When through his illuminating power we fix our eyes on the beauty of the image of the unseen God, and through the image are led up to the more than beautiful vision of the archetype, his Spirit of knowledge is somehow inseparably present. He supplies to those who love to see the truth the power to see the image in himself. He does not make the manifestation from the outside, but in himself leads to knowledge. For, as *no one knows the Father, except the Son* [Matt 11:27], so, *no one is able to say Jesus is Lord, except in the Holy Spirit* [1 Cor 12:3].[72]

In invoking 1 Cor 12:3, Basil points his audience back to the central subject of baptism, for it is this verse that he cites in order to demonstrate that it is the Spirit who enables a human being to make the baptismal confession.[73] The Spirit is thus the means of both this initial confession as well as the believer's increasing knowledge and vision of God.[74] Basil thus provides the Spirit with a distinct identity and purpose as well as ensures that the Spirit is indivisible and inseparable from the Father and the Son.

We leave this overview of Basil's pneumatology, then, having brought together many of the distinctive themes explored in the pre-Nicene period.

---

69. *Spir.* 18.45. On this passage, see further Behr, *Nicene Faith*, 2:306–8.

70. See Hildebrand, *Trinitarian Theology*, 180–81.

71. Haykin, *Pneumatomachian Controversy*, 127.

72. *Spir.* 18.47. On this passage, see further Behr, *Nicene Faith*, 2:312–13.

73. See *Spir.* 11.27, 16.38; Haykin, *Pneumatomachian Controversy*, 128.

74. Haykin, *Pneumatomachian Controversy*, 129.

For here we have nothing less than a glorious vision of how the Spirit, as a distinct divine person who has operated throughout all of salvation history, not only testifies to and reveals the Father and the Son but also, in so doing, reveals his own divinity. By appealing to the liturgy of the church, with special attention to the baptismal confession, Basil connects his ideas about the Spirit with not just the Scriptures but also the lived experience of Christians. In sum, while his apologetic purposes constrain him from saying so explicitly, Basil is making clear, in a creative and powerful way, that the Spirit is nothing less than God.

Basil and Pre-Nicene Pneumatology

As suggested above, Basil indeed draws upon and ties together many of the key pre-Nicene pneumatological themes that have been studied in this book. Thus, though his particular polemical context and his expanded appeal to the liturgical tradition of the church prevent Basil from addressing these themes in as much detail as we observed in the writings of Athanasius and Didymus, it is nevertheless the case that he presents the Spirit as testifying to the deity and lordship of the other divine persons,[75] and he portrays the Spirit as not only having been active in the Old Testament period but also having ministered to the angels and the hosts of heaven from the time of their creation.[76] Likewise, Basil at times applies the term "person" (*prosōpon*) to the members of the Trinity,[77] and as described above has an expansive vision of how the Spirit reveals the divine economy and brings humanity into the life of the Godhead.[78] Having already examined the development of these themes in Athanasius and Didymus, we will rather focus on how Basil can illuminate one other vitally important aspect of pre-Nicene pneumatology to which we have not given as much attention thus far in this chapter: the experience of the Holy Spirit.

---

75. See, e.g., *Spir.* 16.38 (drawing on 1 Cor 12:3) and 18.46 (John 16:14).

76. See *Spir.* 16.38–39.

77. Presumably, the Spirit is included in the reference at *Spir.* 30.77 if not at *Spir.* 5.8 or 18.45. While not meeting the criteria to count as an instance of prosopological exegesis, Basil's reading of 2 Thess 3:5 at *Spir.* 21.52 to identify the Spirit as the "Lord" being spoken of is suggestive of earlier efforts to identify the "Lord" in texts such as Ps 110:1.

78. Besides *Spir.* 18.47, quoted above, see also *Spir.* 9.23, 15.36, 16.38, 24.56. See further Ayres, *Nicaea and Its Legacy*, 219.

Throughout the chapters of this book devoted to the pre-Nicene period, we observed that the lived experience of the Spirit was a major point of emphasis in the first centuries of the Christian movement. One might wonder, then, if the transition into the post-Nicene, post-Constantinian world had turned the Spirit into a theological abstraction rather than the beating heart of Christian life and worship. Basil is a particularly helpful guide in pursuing this line of inquiry. As one committed to the ascetic life, Basil had a profound experience of the Holy Spirit, and it was perhaps this that in part motivated his defense of the Spirit's full divinity; as Haykin writes, "The fact of Basil's (and many of his contemporaries') living experience of the Spirit is overlooked by those scholars who regard him (and the other theologians of his day) as simply a philosopher in ecclesiastical garb."[79] Though Basil does not seem to be particularly interested in some of the traditional markers of charismatic enthusiasm, we should not therefore overlook the ways in which he did envision the Christian life as Spirit-filled. For Basil, this experience of the Spirit is particularly manifested in the act of spiritual vision or contemplation (*theōria*). Proceeding from Paul's image of Moses and the veil (2 Cor 3:12–18), Basil suggests that this spiritual vision is not only necessary to correctly interpret the Old Testament, but also to behold the Spirit himself:

> For, as those things that are near brilliant colors are themselves colored because of the rays of light that flow around them, so he who clearly fixes his eyes on the Spirit is somehow transformed by the Spirit's glory into something brighter as his heart is illuminated by the truth of the Spirit, as if by a light. And this is the transformation from the glory of the Spirit to his own glory; it does not happen in any insignificant or faint way, but in a manner that is suitable for one who is enlightened by the Spirit.[80]

The Spirit, then, enlightens, illuminates, and transforms, and is both the means and the end of spiritual contemplation. As Ayres comments, "Thus the contemplation of the Spirit necessary to understand the Spirit is itself at the core of the Christian life, and through the work of the Spirit in the believer this contemplation is enabled."[81] By extension, the Chris-

---

79. Haykin, *Pneumatomachian Controversy*, 25 n. 81; cf. ibid., 24–25.

80. *Spir.* 21.52.

81. Ayres, *Nicaea and Its Legacy*, 219; cf. Wilken, "Spirit of Holiness," 84–85.

tian can "see" the Father and the Son; the unstated but clear implication, of course, is that the Spirit is himself God.[82]

Having arrived at this point we shift our attention to the end of the Pneumatomachian controversy and the explicit declaration that the Spirit is God, looking briefly at Gregory of Nazianzus and then the Council of Constantinople in 381.

After Basil: Gregory of Nazianzus and the Council of Constantinople

Basil died in 379, not long after writing *On the Holy Spirit* and on the eve of the conclusion to the Pneumatomachian controversy. For it was later in this same year that Theodosius, an ally of the pro-Nicene cause, became emperor, and Gregory of Nazianzus, Basil's Cappadocian contemporary, was sent to Constantinople to bolster the pro-Nicene cause.[83] In 380, Gregory preached a series of five orations that set out his trinitarian theology. In what would come to be called his *Fifth Theological Oration*, Gregory turned his focus to the Holy Spirit.[84] Towards the end of his sermon, having covered much of the same ground that Basil had, Gregory draws the following key conclusion in the form of a dialogue between himself and an interlocutor:

> *What, then? Is the Spirit God?*
>
> Certainly.
>
> *Is he consubstantial?*
>
> Yes, if he is God.[85]

Emboldened by the change in political and therefore theological circumstances, Gregory thus made explicit what Basil, who had still been hoping to win over the Pneumatomachians, had left implicit. The Godhead is one, and yet this one God exists eternally as Father, Son, and Spirit, who are united on account of sharing a common substance.[86]

82. See Ayres, *Nicaea and Its Legacy*, 219–20.

83. See Ayres, *Nicaea and Its Legacy*, 240–42; Behr, *Nicene Faith*, 2:327.

84. For overview of this text and its argument, see Behr, *Nicene Faith*, 2:360–70.

85. *Orat.* 31.10; translation from Williams and Wickham, *On God and Christ*. See also Behr, *Nicene Faith*, 2:363–64.

86. See *Orat.* 31.17–19. On the trinitarian theology of Gregory of Nazianzus more generally, see Ayres, *Nicaea and Its Legacy*, 244–51.

In the following year, 381, Theodosius called a council in Constantinople. Basil's ideas concerning the Spirit, having been further defended and developed by Gregory of Nazianzus, played an influential role in the drafting of the creed produced by that council.[87] Whereas the Nicene Creed simply stated belief "in the Holy Spirit," the Creed of Constantinople affirms more extensively belief "in the Holy Spirit, the Lord and Life-giver, who proceeds from the Father who is worshipped and glorified together with the Father and the Son, who spoke by the prophets."[88] In this Niceno-Constantinopolitan Creed, then, we have a satisfactory summation of Basil's view of the Holy Spirit, affirming the Spirit as fully divine, a coequal member of the Trinity. Whether the affirmation was implicit, as in Basil and the creed, or explicit, as in Gregory of Nazianzus, it was clear that the Spirit was, at last, God.

Conclusion

In this chapter, we have considered how Athanasius of Alexandria, Didymus the Blind, and Basil of Caesarea argued for the full divinity of the Holy Spirit in the context of the Pneumatomachian controversy. Athanasius broke a long tradition of subordinationism in affirming the coequality of the Spirit with the Father and the Son, emphasizing the unity of action and identity in the Trinity. That being said, Athanasius' account of how the three divine *hypostases* should be distinguished remained somewhat underdeveloped, opening the door for further pneumatological reflection. For his part, Didymus also explored the notion of the Trinity's unity of substance and activity through his emphasis on the inseparable operations of the three divine persons. Didymus, though, clarifies the distinct identity of the Holy Spirit on account of the particularity of his mission with respect to the work of sanctification. Finally, Basil built on these earlier writings to advance his own case for the full divinity of the Spirit; in particular, he takes some of the liturgical arguments related to the Spirit's role at baptism and extends them to give the worship and tradition of the church a greater degree of prominence in his theological method. For each of these writers,

87. See Hildebrand, *On the Holy Spirit*, 21. On the Council of Constantinople and its creed, see further Ayres, *Nicaea and Its Legacy*, 253–60; Behr, *Nicene Faith*, 2:370–79.

88. Translation from Ayres, *Nicaea and Its Legacy*, 255. The canons of the council also formally anathematized the Pneumatomachians; see further Behr, *Nicene Faith*, 2:370–71.

it is clear that some of the major themes of pre-Nicene pneumatology, such as the Spirit's provision of divine testimony, role in constructing Christian identity, association with person-language, and revelation of the divine economy, were creatively retrieved and developed by these pro-Nicene figures in ways that were appropriate for their new circumstances. Likewise, the exegesis of the Scriptures and the experience of the Spirit remained important concerns and motivators for defending the deity of the Holy Spirit, even as the nature of this experience increasingly took on an ascetic cast. As a result of this complex and creative process, full of both continuities and discontinuities with previous pneumatological reflection, the church was able to articulate a fully-formed trinitarian theology in which the Holy Spirit was understood to be fully divine.

Our mosaic of early Christian pneumatology is now complete; at last, the full divinity of the Spirit is in view. Customarily, this is what visitors to the mosaic focus on, taking in the beauty, creativity, and lasting significance of these tiles set in the post-Nicene period. Our study, however, has demonstrated that it is in fact those interior tiles, faint from age and, at times, neglect, that in fact inspired these most recent additions to the mosaic. We also are now in position to spot some key continuities from the earliest to the latest of the tiles placed in the mosaic; for instance, we note that all of them, without exception, are primarily made of the same raw material, which is *the interpretation of the Scriptures*. Likewise, we can observe that each and every tile is adhered to the wall with the glue of the *lived experience of the Holy Spirit* in the Christian community. Not only, then, can we see the finished composition displaying the Spirit as God, but we have made significant steps in understanding the process by which the master craftsmen, from the writers of the New Testament onward, created this mosaic. As we take one final glance at the mosaic, we are not surprised to find that later artists continued to develop some of the colors and patterns from this central image as theological reflection on the person and work of the Holy Spirit has continued, even into the present day. While these further elaborations and embellishments are a worthy subject for another time, we have now seen what we have come here to see. The Spirit is, indeed, God.

CHAPTER 7

The Invitation of the Holy Spirit

Aswe noted at the very outset of this book, the Christian doctrine of the Trinity has perplexed artists and iconographers no less than pastors and theologians, with the depiction of the Holy Spirit proving a particularly challenging task. Whereas some images of the Trinity, like the one with which we opened this book, portray the Spirit as a dove, suggesting a lack of personhood relative to the embodied forms of the Father and the Son, other iconography has been more successful in portraying the Holy Spirit as a distinct divine person. Arguably the most famous such representation of the Trinity is that of Andrei Rublev (ca. 1370–1430), whose icon depicting the Trinity according to the scene known as "The Hospitality of Abraham" (Gen 18:1–16) has been celebrated as "a theologically correct and aesthetically perfect image of the Holy Trinity."[1] In this icon, Father, Son, and Spirit appear in the form of three angels seated around an altar on which sits a chalice containing the head of a sacrificed calf. Crucially, the angels themselves are portrayed identically, in the same style and size, holding the same staves, sitting on the same seats or thrones, and wearing the same kinds of garments. The implication, of course, is that the three divine persons share a single substance or essence; there is no hint that the Holy Spirit is in any way subordinate to or less personal than the Father or the Son. There is, however, still distinction made between the three divine persons, with Rublev using color and positioning to draw attention to their distinctive identities. In reading the icon from left to right, we find the Holy Spirit at the right of the image, third in sequence as appropriate for the

---

1. Yazykova and Luka, "Theological Principles of the Icon," 19. This description of the icon and its significance follows that of Bunge, *Rublev Trinity*, 94–107. A brief summary of this approach to trinitarian iconography can be found in Cavarnos, *Byzantine Iconography*, 2:61–64.

third person of the Trinity. There, the Spirit sits wearing blue and green clothing, corresponding, respectively, to his divinity and his work as the giver of life. Like the Son, the Spirit inclines his head and directs his gaze towards the Father. His left arm is exposed, as is the right arm of the Son, suggesting Irenaeus' teaching on the Son and the Spirit as the "two hands" of God. The Son points to the Spirit, and the Father directs both his gaze and his right hand of blessing to the Spirit, suggesting that Rublev's focal point was actually not the Son, who is at the physical center of the icon, but the Spirit, and on this basis it has been argued that the scene in view is actually that of the Johannine Pentecost (John 20:19–22):

> The movement between the three divine persons, the intra-trinitarian conversation, proceeds from the Son: With entreaty he looks at the Father, while his right hand points to the chalice of his Passion and beyond that to the Spirit. This look and this gesture intimate the request for the sending of the Paraclete, which only becomes possible through the self-sacrifice of the Son. The Father, who always hears the son (Jn 11:42), fulfills this request: His gaze is directed to the Spirit, who is enthroned with him behind the altar table, and his right hand bestows on him the blessing for this completion of the saving work of the Son. The Holy Spirit, however, bows his head in humble assent, which is shown by his lowered right hand.[2]

It is fitting, then, that this magisterial artistic achievement that best portrays the Spirit as a distinct divine person proceeds from the same Paraclete passages that this book argued initiated the trajectory of ascribing distinct personhood to the Spirit.

Perhaps most intriguing is how this icon, by leaving open a space at the front of the table, invites us to join the circle, and join the life of the triune God. The implication is that in light of Pentecost, and the personal indwelling of the Holy Spirit, we are extended the invitation to participate in God's own life; Rublev is trying to communicate, in other words, that "a life in communion with the All-holy Trinity in and through the Holy Spirit is the meaning and end of the Christian life."[3] Accordingly, the Rublev icon challenges us to think of the Holy Spirit not as an impersonal dove, but as a distinct, coequal divine person, who invites us into God's own life. We will return to this subject of the invitation of the Spirit shortly, but first we must

2. Bunge, *Rublev Icon*, 105.

3. Bunge, *Rublev Icon*, 77.

briefly recapitulate the main claims of this book and consider some of the scholarly implications that follow from its conclusions.

Summary and Significance

In a sense, this book has given the long-range story of how the theology behind the Rublev icon came to be, for we have traced the process by which the Christians of the first four centuries came to affirm the fundamental principles of the view of the Holy Spirit captured in this famous depiction of the Trinity. At its core, this book has argued that Christians of the patristic period, in light of their lived experience of the Holy Spirit, came to identify this Spirit as a distinct divine person alongside the Father and the Son as a result of careful reflection on Scripture. In tracing movements towards ascribing personhood and divinity to the Holy Spirit in the pre-Nicene period, we identified four key themes that, emerging from biblical exegesis, created the foundation for the later orthodox doctrine of the Holy Spirit. In the aftermath of Pentecost, the early believers' reflection on the Scriptures and their experience of the Spirit resulted in new approaches to understanding the person and work of the Spirit. One of the most significant of these for the long-term development of early Christian pneumatology was the Johannine presentation of the Spirit as the Paraclete who is the source of divine testimony to the true nature of Jesus' person and work. As some of these believers began to construct Christianity as a religion increasingly distinct from Judaism, there arose a lively debate concerning to whom this Spirit belonged, be it Jews or Christians. As argued by the Epistle of Barnabas, the Spirit that Christians experienced at baptism was in fact the same Spirit who had been active among the Jews prior to the coming of Christ and who was from the beginning the Spirit of the Son. Building on this theme, Justin Martyr denied the Spirit to the Jews of his day, insisting that the Spirit had been transferred to the church, which was the true Israel. Justin was also significant in launching a highly significant trajectory of pneumatological development that would contribute to the understanding of the personhood of the Spirit. Utilizing an ancient person-centered reading strategy that scholars call prosopological exegesis, Justin interpreted Old Testament dialogical passages in such a way as to portray the Spirit as able to speak in the divine theodrama as his own "person" (*prosōpon*) for the purpose of providing testimony to the deity and lordship of the Father and the Son. While Irenaeus refined this basic approach, it was ultimately

Tertullian whose emerging trinitarian theology allowed him to move this understanding of the Spirit's personhood out of the theatrical or literary spheres and apply it to a claim about the internal dynamics of the triune God, paving the way for person-language to become the most powerful metaphor for understanding diversity within the Godhead. Irenaeus and Tertullian were noteworthy not just for their contribution to the emerging personhood of the Spirit, but also for their portrayal of the Spirit's work in revealing the divine economy. While these writers thereby contributed to our understanding of the distinctive mission of the Spirit in revealing the mysteries of God to humanity, the most significant development came from Origen, who expanded upon this theme in more detail by positing that the Spirit was eternally present with the Father and the Son. Though this affirmation provided support for pro-Nicene writers who sought to defend the full divinity of the Holy Spirit, the subordinationist view of the Spirit characteristic of Origen and his predecessors would be fodder for those "Spirit-fighters" opposed to such a move. During the Pneumatomachian crisis of the second half of the fourth century, then, it would fall to Athanasius, Didymus, and Basil of Caesarea to synthesize these key pre-Nicene developments and build on them to weave their arguments for the Spirit's full divinity. Appealing to the unity of action and identity in the Trinity as well as the liturgical tradition of the church with respect to baptism, these pro-Nicene figures articulated a fully-formed trinitarian theology in which the Holy Spirit was understood to be fully divine. Thus, by 381, the Holy Spirit was recognized as a coequal member of the Trinity, distinguished from the Father and the Son not on the basis of his relative level of authority or glory but simply on account of the nature of his origin. While the lack of a precise account of the Spirit's procession would, of course, be the source of continuing, and indeed contentious, pneumatological reflection, the basic contours of trinitarian theology were in place. Throughout, we have found that it was reflection on the Scriptures (primarily, that is, the Old Testament) and on the continued experience of the Spirit that provided the essential context for the development of early Christian pneumatology.

This book has sought to contribute to scholarly understanding of the development of early Christian pneumatology by going beyond a mere survey of different patristic writers' teachings on the Holy Spirit to considering how reflection on Scripture and the experience of the Spirit motivated the creation of certain key themes that would ultimately contribute to the Spirit being recognized as a distinct, fully divine person. It was, I contend, *biblical interpretation and the experience of the Spirit that were the primary drivers of the developing doctrine of the Holy Spirit*, although the liturgical tradition of the church played an important supplemental role towards the end of this process. Specifically, then, this book challenges the prevailing scholarly narrative of the development of early Christian pneumatology, which tends to ignore or marginalize the contributions of pre-Nicene theologians. It was, in fact, figures such as Justin, Irenaeus, Tertullian, and Origen whose biblical exegesis led to instrumental developments regarding the Spirit's provision of divine testimony, role in the construction of Christian identity, association with person-language, and work in revealing the divine economy. While it is true that the most sustained and narrowly focused works on the Spirit date to the post-Nicene period, I have endeavored to show that these arguments clearly build upon earlier pneumatological innovations even as they respond to the new circumstances in which they find themselves.

With respect to the reimagined account of the development of early Christian pneumatology offered by Ayres and Barnes, summarized in the introduction of this book, the argument I have set out herein has affirmed their understanding of this process as a complex story of adaptation, abandonment, and retrieval of earlier pneumatological traditions by later Christian writers. Likewise, Ayres and Barnes were correct to emphasize how this story unfolded in light of early Christian writers' reflection on the meaning of Scripture. That being said, this book has identified significant continuities between figures such as Irenaeus, on the one hand, and, on the other, Tertullian and Origen. Part of the schema of Ayres and Barnes is to place Irenaeus in a different stage of development from Tertullian and Origen, but we have seen that with respect to significant ideas such as their use of prosopological exegesis or their portrayal of the Spirit's revelation of the divine economy, there is profound continuity among these figures. Moreover, by focusing nearly exclusively on how Jewish-Christian pneumatological ideas were rejected or retrieved, Ayres and Barnes neglect to consider how other sources of theology played important roles in this overall process of doctrinal development. This book, then, has aimed at giving a broader account of the development of early Christian pneumatology, considering a wider range of theological innovations in order to explain the historical process by which the Spirit "became" God. We are now in position to return to the invitation of the Spirit.

The Invitation of the Spirit

While this book has clarified that, current popular Christian beliefs not-withstanding, the distinct personhood and full divinity of the Holy Spirit is indeed a non-negotiable element of orthodox Christian theology, we still must reckon with the question of how then we are to engage with the person of the Spirit. In this concluding section, we seek to pull together some of the pneumatological ideas found in this book to help us consider what our response should be to the invitation of the Spirit, as so beautifully communicated by Rublev in his famous icon.

As a first principle, we must begin with the recognition, as we have seen throughout this book, that the lived experience of the Spirit was a hallmark of Christian discipleship. While it would be impossible to adequately account for all of the diversity of approaches to the spiritual life in the first four centuries of Christianity, we can nevertheless identify some core concerns of these church fathers on what it meant for them to live in the Spirit. Central to writers as early as Irenaeus and Tertullian was the belief that the Spirit reveals the divine economy, enabling us to correctly understand the truth about God. While this truth may have initially been received primarily through direct prophecy, by the middle of the third century is has become clear that the normative method of receiving this truth was through the words of the Spirit-inspired Scripture, giving rise to attempts, such as that of Origen, to articulate an appropriate spiritual method of reading the Word of God. Indeed, for Origen the Spirit's work in revealing the divine economy is not merely a matter of transmitting theological information; rather, it is a way of shaping and forming us now, in this life, as people who can have faith amidst all circumstances. Likewise, for Didymus the Holy Spirit makes the knowledge of God an enacted reality, allowing believers to participate in Christ. Drawing together a lot of these threads, Basil of Caesarea envisions the Spirit-filled life as one in which Christians acquire the spiritual vision necessary to rightly read Scripture and, ultimately, to behold God himself. In other words, in the early church fathers there is a consistent recognition that the Spirit leads believers into all truth, but that this truth (given its relationship to Christ, who is the Truth) is inescapably participatory and transformative.

This brings us, then, to the essential question: how does one go about experiencing the Spirit, responding to his invitation in such a way that our lives are transformed and we come to acquire vision of God? Again,

Basil is a worthy guide. In a letter to his friend Gregory of Nazianzus, Basil writes the following:

> We must strive after a quiet mind. As well might the eye ascertain an object put before it while it is wandering restless up and down and sideways, without fixing a steady gaze upon it, as a mind, distracted by a thousand worldly cares, be able clearly to apprehend the truth. . . . Now solitude is of the greatest use for this purpose, inasmuch as it stills our passions, and gives room for principle to cut them out of the soul. . . . Quiet, then, as I have said, is the first step of our sanctification; the tongue purified from the gossip of the world; the eyes unexcited by fair color or comely shape; the ear not relaxing the tone or mind by voluptuous songs, nor by that special mischief, the talk of light men and jesters. Thus the mind, saved from dissipation from without, and not through the senses thrown upon the world, falls back upon itself, and thereby ascends to the contemplation of God.[4]

In other words, if we want to contemplate God (which Basil assumes to be the ultimate end of the Christian life), we must first purify our minds so they are made capable of perceiving God. This process can only take place, Basil insists, if we first engage with the discipline of solitude. As Robert Louis Wilken summarizes, "If the spiritual life is primarily a matter of growth in personal holiness, the Fathers concluded that one should cultivate man's capacity to deal with the obstacles which stand in the way of growth. For this reason Basil dwells at length on the discipline required to achieve this end and the means to be employed in overcoming obstacles."[5] This is, of course, what the church fathers called *ascesis*, a life of discipline in which one pursues the holiness that provides the means of journeying towards God. With this in mind, Basil, as a representative of the church fathers more generally, offers us two challenges by which we can better conceive of responding to the invitation of the Spirit.

First, Basil assumes that the character of the Spirit is such that he is, in effect, what Dale Bruner calls the "shy member of the Trinity."[6] Taking seriously the Spirit's personal identity, Basil exhorts us to make space to respond to the Spirit's invitation, allowing a relationship with him to begin so that he can grow us in holiness and therefore in our ability to contemplate

---

4. *Ep.* 2.2 (trans. *NPNF*).

5. Wilken, "Spirit of Holiness," 82.

6. Bruner and Hordern, *Shy Member of the Trinity*. On the "elusiveness of the Spirit," see further Cole, *He Who Gives Life*, 41–58.

God. We simply cannot expect the Spirit to do this work in us apart from intentional engagement with him, in the same way as careful attention is required to cultivate any other meaningful relationship. My sense of what we need, then, is to expand our conception of what we mean by the term "charismatic." In the North American context in which I write, this word tends to be associated with certain gifts of the Spirit, such as prophecy or speaking in tongues. As we have seen in this book, these manifestations of the outpouring of the Spirit were indeed central to many early Christians' experience of the Spirit, as they are for many believers today. And yet Basil, among other church fathers studied in this book, is perhaps calling us to think about an aspect of the Spirit-filled life that is less emphasized in our time and place. A more fully-orbed conception of a truly Christian charismatic will account for *both* the gifts of the Spirit *and* the cultivation of an intentional relationship with this shy God, pursuing *ascesis* and the development of an inner life from which will overflow the fruit of holiness. It seems to me that the most urgent and most significant task of this generation is to recover, amidst a culture that prizes speed and efficiency, and amidst a world that ceaselessly clamors for our constant attention through new digital technologies, a way of life that allows us to set aside the distractions of this world in order to ascend to God. Surely no other task would be as counter-cultural or as compelling to those who are exhausted from their pursuit of these virtues of the world. For Basil, cultivating this solitude meant actually removing himself from "the world," carving out a monastic life far from any urban center, though even he admitted that the solitary life in and of itself was not enough to place him on the road to holiness.[7] For us, we must consider how, unless we are willing to follow Basil in seeking to give up the active life for the contemplative one, we can still find ways to quiet our minds and be filled with the Spirit, in the places that God has us now.

Second, Basil reminds us that this expanded notion of being "charismatic" is not synonymous with spontaneity or freedom from tradition or authority. Basil, of course, developed his defense of the full deity of the Holy Spirit in response to a liturgical issue and on the basis of the church's tradition of worship. More broadly, his concern for the Spirit-filled life in no way appeared to conflict with his passion for theological precision or liturgical propriety. What this suggests is that the charismatic and liturgical streams of Christianity in fact need one another. If charismatic Christianity without liturgical Christianity is ahistorical chaos, and if liturgical Christianity

7. See *Ep.* 2.1.

without charismatic Christianity is a bloated corpse, Basil and the church fathers show us that the church needs both the tradition of worship that itself gave rise to fundamental theological principles as well as the filling of the Spirit that makes us alive, increases our holiness, and enables us to contemplate God.[8] The words spoken at baptism, the words pronounced in the worship of the church, the words of Scripture—all these things both point to the truth about the Holy Spirit as a distinct divine person and call us to hearken to the still, small voice of this same Spirit who seeks to draw us into relationship with himself, not simply for our own salvation, but for his purposes of mission and renewal in the world. A true charismatic, therefore, is one who encounters and engages with the Spirit in a way that stands under the teaching of the church and its Scriptures while also allowing the Spirit to breathe new life wherever dry bones may be found.

This, then, is the invitation of the Spirit: to make space in our lives for the Spirit's life-giving breath to create in us the very character of Christ, by which we may one day behold God face-to-face. And, in the face of such an immense, awe-inspiring invitation, we can only begin with prayer: *Veni, Creator Spiritus* . . . .

8. On so-called "three streams" approaches to Christianity, which also include the evangelical emphasis on a personal relationship with God and the need to share one's faith, see Bevins, *Ever Ancient, Ever New*, 141–54.

Bibliography

Primary Sources

The Ante-Nicene Fathers: Translations of the Writings of the Fathers Down to A.D. 325. Edited by Alexander Roberts and James Donaldson. 1885–87. 10 vols. Reprint, Peabody, MA: Hendrickson, 1994.

Barnard, Leslie William, trans. *St. Justin Martyr: The First and Second Apologies.* Ancient Christian Writers 56. New York: Paulist, 1997.

Behr, John, ed. and trans. *Origen: On First Principles.* 2 vols. Oxford Early Christian Texts. Oxford: Oxford University Press, 2017.

Behr, John, trans. *St Irenaeus of Lyons: On the Apostolic Preaching.* Popular Patristics Series 17. Crestwood, NY: St Vladimir's Seminary Press, 1997.

DelCogliano, Mark, Andrew Radde-Gallwitz, and Lewis Ayres, trans. *Works on the Spirit: Athanasius the Great and Didymus the Blind.* Popular Patristics Series 43. Yonkers, NY: St Vladimir's Seminary Press, 2011.

Evans, Ernest, ed. and trans. *Tertullian's Treatise against Praxeas: The Text Edited, with an Introduction, Translation, and Commentary.* 1948. Reprint, Eugene, OR: Wipf and Stock, 2011.

Falls, Thomas B., trans. *St. Justin Martyr: Dialogue with Trypho.* Revised by Thomas P. Halton. Edited by Michael Slusser. Selections from the Fathers of the Church 3. Washington, DC: The Catholic University of America Press, 2003.

Heine, Ronald E, trans. *Origen: Commentary on the Gospel according to John, Books 13–32.* The Fathers of the Church 89. Washington, DC: The Catholic University of America Press, 1993.

Hildebrand, Stephen, trans. *St Basil the Great: On the Holy Spirit.* Popular Patristics Series 42. Yonkers, NY: St Vladimir's Seminary Press, 2011.

Holmes, Michael W., ed. and trans. *The Apostolic Fathers: Greek Texts and English Translations.* 3rd ed. Grand Rapids: Baker Academic, 2007.

A Select Library of Nicene and Post-Nicene Fathers of the Christian Church. Edited by Philip Schaff and Henry Wace. 28 vols. in 2 series. 1886–89. Reprint, Peabody, MA: Hendrickson, 1996.

Steenberg, M. C. Irenaeus, ed. and rev. *St. Irenaeus of Lyons: Against the Heresies, Book 3.* Translated by Dominic J. Unger. Ancient Christian Writers 64. New York: Newman, 2012.

Williams, Frederick, and Lionel Wickham, trans. *St Gregory of Nazianzus: On God and Christ—The Five Theological Orations and Two Letters to Cledonius*. Popular Patristics Series 23. Crestwood, NY: St Vladimir's Seminary Press, 2002.

Secondary Sources

Albl, Martin C. *"And Scripture Cannot Be Broken": The Form and Function of the Early Christian* Testimonia *Collections*. Supplements to Novum Testamentum 46. Leiden: Brill, 1999.

Allert, Craig D. *Revelation, Truth, Canon and Interpretation: Studies in Justin Martyr's Dialogue with Trypho*. Supplements to Vigiliae Christianae 64. Leiden: Brill, 2002.

Anatolios, Khaled. *Athanasius*. The Early Church Fathers. London: Routledge, 2004.

———. *Retrieving Nicaea: The Development and Meaning of Trinitarian Doctrine*. Grand Rapids: Baker Academic, 2011.

Andresen, Carl. "Zur Entstehung und Geschichte des trinitarischen Personbegriffes." *Zeitschrift für die neutestamentliche Wissenschaft und die Kunde der älteren Kirche* 52 (1961) 1–39.

Aune, David E. *Prophecy in Early Christianity and the Ancient Mediterranean World*. Grand Rapids: Eerdmans, 1983.

Ayres, Lewis. "The Holy Spirit as the 'Undiminished Giver': Didymus the Blind's *De Spiritu Sancto* and the Development of Nicene Pneumatology." In *The Holy Spirit in the Fathers of the Church: The Proceedings of the Seventh International Patristics Conference, Maynooth, 2008*, edited by D. Vincent Twomey and Janet E. Rutherford, 57–72. Dublin: Four Courts, 2010.

———. "Innovation and *Ressourcement* in Pro-Nicene Pneumatology." *Augustinian Studies* 39 (2008) 187–206.

———. *Nicaea and Its Legacy: An Approach to Fourth-Century Trinitarian Theology*. Oxford: Oxford University Press, 2004.

———. "*Spiritus Amborum*: Augustine and Pro-Nicene Pneumatology." *Augustinian Studies* 39 (2008) 207–21.

Ayres, Lewis, and Michel René Barnes. "Pneumatology: Historical and Methodological Considerations." *Augustinian Studies* 39 (2008) 163–236.

Barnes, Michel René. "Augustine's Last Pneumatology." *Augustinian Studies* 39 (2008) 223–34.

———. "The Beginning and End of Early Christian Pneumatology." *Augustinian Studies* 39 (2008) 169–86.

———. "Irenaeus's Trinitarian Theology." *Nova et Vetera* 7 (2009) 67–106.

Barnes, Timothy David. *Tertullian: A Historical and Literary Study*. Oxford: Clarendon, 1971.

Barrett, C. K. *A Commentary on the First Epistle to the Corinthians*. Black's New Testament Commentaries. London: Black, 1968.

———. *The Gospel according to St. John*. 2nd ed. Philadelphia: Westminster, 1978.

Bates, Matthew W. *The Birth of the Trinity: Jesus, God, and Spirit in New Testament and Early Christian Interpretations of the Old Testament*. Oxford: Oxford University Press, 2015.

———. *The Hermeneutics of the Apostolic Proclamation: The Center of Paul's Method of Scriptural Interpretation*. Waco, TX: Baylor University Press, 2012.

Beeley, Christopher A., and Mark E. Weedman, "Introduction: The Study of Early Christian Biblical Interpretation." In *The Bible and Early Trinitarian Theology*, edited by Christopher A. Beeley and Mark E. Weedman, 1–26. CUA Studies in Early Christianity. Washington, DC: The Catholic University of America Press, 2018.

Behr, John. *Asceticism and Anthropology in Irenaeus and Clement*. Oxford Early Christian Studies. Oxford: Oxford University Press, 2000.

———. *The Nicene Faith*. Vol. 2 of *Formation of Christian Theology*. 2 vols. Crestwood, NY: St Vladimir's Seminary Press, 2004.

———. *The Way to Nicaea*. Vol. 1 of *Formation of Christian Theology*. Crestwood, NY: St Vladimir's Seminary Press, 2001.

Bekken, Per Jarle. *The Lawsuit Motif in John's Gospel from New Perspectives: Jesus Christ, Crucified Criminal and Emperor of the World*. Supplements to Novum Testamentum 158. Leiden: Brill, 2015.

Bethune-Baker, J. F. *An Introduction to the Early History of Christian Doctrine: To the Time of the Council of Chalcedon*. 2nd ed. London: Methuen, 1920.

Bevins, Winfield. *Ever Ancient, Ever New: The Allure of Liturgy for a New Generation*. Grand Rapids: Zondervan, 2019.

Bird, Michael F., et al. *How God Became Jesus*. Grand Rapids: Zondervan, 2014.

Blowers, Paul M. *The Drama of the Divine Economy: Creator and Creation in Early Christian Theology and Piety*. Oxford Early Christian Studies. Oxford: Oxford University Press, 2012.

Boyarin, Daniel. *Border Lines: The Partition of Judaeo-Christianity*. Divinations. Philadelphia: University of Pennsylvania Press, 2004.

Breck, John. *Spirit of Truth: The Origins of Johannine Pneumatology*. Vol. 1 of *Spirit of Truth: The Holy Spirit in Johannine Tradition*. Crestwood, NY: St Vladimir's Seminary Press, 1991.

Briggman, Anthony. *Irenaeus of Lyons and the Theology of the Holy Spirit*. Oxford Early Christian Studies. Oxford: Oxford University Press, 2012.

———. "Literary and Rhetorical Theory in Irenaeus, Part 1." *Vigiliae Christianae* 69 (2015) 500–527.

———. "Measuring Justin's Approach to the Spirit: Trinitarian Conviction and Binitarian Orientation." *Vigiliae Christianae* 63 (2009) 107–37.

Brown, Raymond E. *The Gospel according to John XIII–XXI*. Anchor Bible 29A. Garden City, NY: Doubleday, 1970.

Brown, Tricia Gates. *Spirit in the Writings of John: Johannine Pneumatology in Social-Scientific Perspective*. Journal for the Study of the New Testament Supplement Series 253. London: T&T Clark, 2003.

Bruner, Frederick Dale, and William Hordern. *The Holy Spirit: Shy Member of the Trinity*. Minneapolis: Augsburg Fortress, 1984.

Bucur, Bogdan G. *Angelomorphic Pneumatology: Clement of Alexandria and Other Early Christian Witnesses*. Supplements to Vigiliae Christianae 95. Leiden: Brill, 2009.

Bunge, Gabriel. *The Rublev Trinity: The Icon of the Trinity by the Monk-Painter Andrei Rublev*. Translated by Andrew Louth. Crestwood, NY: St Vladimir's Seminary Press, 2007.

Burge, Gary M. *The Anointed Community: The Holy Spirit in the Johannine Tradition*. Grand Rapids: Eerdmans, 1987.

Burgess, Stanley M. *The Holy Spirit: Ancient Christian Traditions*. Peabody, MA: Hendrickson, 1984.

Burns, J. Patout, Jr., and Robin M. Jensen. *Christianity in Roman Africa: The Development of Its Practices and Beliefs*. Grand Rapids: Eerdmans, 2014.

Carleton Paget, James. *The Epistle of Barnabas*. Wissenschaftliche Untersuchungen zum Neuen Testament 2/64. Tübingen: Mohr Siebeck, 1994.

Carson, D. A. *The Gospel according to John*. Pillar New Testament Commentary. Grand Rapids: Eerdmans, 1991.

Castelo, Daniel. *Pneumatology: A Guide for the Perplexed*. London: Bloomsbury T&T Clark, 2015.

Cavarnos, Constantine. *Guide to Byzantine Iconography*. 2 vols. Boston: Holy Transfiguration Monastery, 1993, 2001.

Chan, Francis. *Forgotten God: Reversing Our Tragic Neglect of the Holy Spirit*. Colorado Springs: David C. Cook, 2009.

Ciampa, Roy E., and Brian S. Rosner. *The First Letter to the Corinthians*. Pillar New Testament Commentary. Grand Rapids: Eerdmans, 2010.

Cole, Graham A. *He Who Gives Life: The Doctrine of the Holy Spirit*. Foundations of Evangelical Theology. Wheaton, IL: Crossway, 2007.

Collins, Paul M. *The Trinity: A Guide for the Perplexed*. London: T&T Clark, 2008.

Collins, Raymond F. *First Corinthians*. Sacra Pagina 7. Collegeville, MN: Liturgical, 1999.

Crouzel, Henri. *Origen*. Translated by A. S. Worrall. San Francisco: Harper and Row, 1989.

Decret, François. *Early Christianity in North Africa*. Translated by Edward L. Smither. Eugene, OR: Cascade, 2009.

DelCogliano, Mark. "Basil of Caesarea, Didymus the Blind, and the Anti-Pneumatomachian Exegesis of Amos 4:14 and John 1:3." *Journal of Theological Studies* 61 (2010) 644–58.

DeSimone, Russell J. "The Holy Spirit according to Novatian *De Trinitate*." *Augustinianum* 10 (1970) 360–87.

———. *The Treatise of Novatian the Roman Presbyter on the Trinity: A Study of the Text and the Doctrine*. Studia Ephemeridis Augustinianum 4. Rome: Institutum Patristicum Augustinianum, 1970.

Dively Lauro, Elizabeth Ann. *The Soul and Spirit of Scripture within Origen's Exegesis*. The Bible in Ancient Christianity 3. Leiden: Brill, 2005.

Dodd, C. H. *According to the Scriptures: The Sub-structure of New Testament Theology*. London: Nisbet, 1952.

Dunn, Geoffrey D. *Tertullian*. The Early Church Fathers. London: Routledge, 2004.

Dunn, James D. G. *Beginning from Jerusalem*. Vol. 2 of *Christianity in the Making*. Grand Rapids: Eerdmans, 2009.

———. *Jesus and the Spirit: A Study of the Religious and Charismatic Experience of Jesus and the First Christians as Reflected in the New Testament*. 1975. Reprint, Grand Rapids: Eerdmans, 1997.

———. *Neither Jew nor Greek: A Contested Identity*. Vol. 3 of *Christianity in the Making*. Grand Rapids: Eerdmans, 2015.

Ehrman, Bart D. *How Jesus Became God: The Exaltation of a Jewish Preacher from Galilee*. New York: HarperOne, 2014.

Emmrich, Martin. "*Pneuma* in Hebrews: Prophet and Interpreter." *Westminster Theological Journal* 63 (2002) 55–71.

Fee, Gordon D. *The First Epistle to the Corinthians*. New International Commentary on the New Testament. Grand Rapids: Eerdmans, 1987.

———. *God's Empowering Presence: The Holy Spirit in the Letters of Paul*. Peabody, MA: Hendrickson, 1994.

Ferguson, Everett. *The Rule of Faith: A Guide.* Cascade Companions 20. Eugene, OR: Cascade, 2015.

Gorman, Michael J. *Apostle of the Crucified Lord: A Theological Introduction to Paul and His Letters.* 2nd ed. Grand Rapids: Eerdmans, 2017.

Grant, Robert M. *Irenaeus of Lyons.* The Early Church Fathers. London: Routledge, 1997.

Gwynn, David M. *Athanasius of Alexandria: Bishop, Theologian, Ascetic, Father.* Christian Theology in Context. Oxford: Oxford University Press, 2012.

Harnack, Adolf. *History of Dogma.* Translated from the 3rd German ed. by Neil Buchanan. 7 vols. Boston: Little, Brown, 1896–1905.

Harvey, A. E. *Jesus on Trial: A Study in the Fourth Gospel.* London: SPCK, 1976.

Hay, David M. *Glory at the Right Hand: Psalm 110 in Early Christianity.* Society of Biblical Literature Monograph Series 18. Nashville: Abingdon, 1973.

Haykin, Michael A. G. *The Exegesis of 1 and 2 Corinthians in the Pneumatomachian Controversy of the Fourth Century.* Supplements to Vigiliae Christianae 27. Leiden: Brill, 1994.

Hays, Richard B. *Echoes of Scripture in the Gospels.* Waco, TX: Baylor University Press, 2016.

———. *Echoes of Scripture in the Letters of Paul.* New Haven: Yale University Press, 1989.

Heine, Ronald E. *Origen: Scholarship in the Service of the Church.* Christian Theology in Context. Oxford: Oxford University Press, 2010.

———. "The Role of the Gospel of John in the Montanist Controversy." *Second Century* 6 (1987) 1–19.

Hicks, Jonathan Douglas. *Trinity, Economy, and Scripture: Recovering Didymus the Blind.* Journal of Theological Interpretation Supplement 12. Winona Lake, IN: Eisenbrauns, 2015.

Hildebrand, Stephen M. *Basil of Caesarea.* Foundations of Theological Exegesis and Christian Spirituality. Grand Rapids: Baker Academic, 2014.

———. *The Trinitarian Theology of Basil of Caesarea: A Synthesis of Greek Thought and Biblical Truth.* Washington, DC: The Catholic University of America Press, 2007.

Hill, Charles E. *The Johannine Corpus in the Early Church.* Oxford: Oxford University Press, 2004.

Holmes, Christopher R. J. *The Holy Spirit.* New Studies in Dogmatics. Grand Rapids: Zondervan, 2015.

Hughes, Kyle R. "The Spirit and the Scriptures: Revisiting Cyprian's Use of Prosopological Exegesis." *Journal of Early Christian History* 8 (2018) 35–48.

———. "The Spirit Speaks: Pneumatological Innovation in the Scriptural Exegesis of Justin and Tertullian." *Vigiliae Christianae* 69 (2015) 463–83.

———. *The Trinitarian Testimony of the Spirit: Prosopological Exegesis and the Development of Pre-Nicene Pneumatology.* Supplements to Vigiliae Christianae 147. Leiden: Brill, 2018.

Hurtado, Larry W. *How on Earth Did Jesus Become a God? Historical Questions about Earliest Devotion to Jesus.* Grand Rapids: Eerdmans, 2005.

———. *Lord Jesus Christ: Devotion to Jesus in Earliest Christianity.* Grand Rapids: Eerdmans, 2003.

Hvalvik, Reidar. *The Struggle for Scripture and Covenant: The Purpose of the Epistle of Barnabas and Jewish-Christian Competition in the Second Century.* Wissenschaftliche Untersuchungen zum Neuen Testament 2/82. Tübingen: Mohr Siebeck, 1996.

Jefford, Clayton N. *Reading the Apostolic Fathers: A Student's Introduction.* 2nd ed. Grand Rapids: Baker Academic, 2012.

Johnson, Luke Timothy. *Hebrews: A Commentary.* New Testament Library. Louisville: Westminster John Knox, 2006.

———. *Religious Experience in Earliest Christianity: A Missing Dimension in New Testament Studies.* Minneapolis: Fortress, 1998.

Juel, Donald. *Messianic Exegesis: Christological Interpretation of the Old Testament in Early Christianity.* Philadelphia: Fortress, 1988.

Kärkkäinen, Veli-Matti. *The Holy Spirit: A Guide to Christian Theology.* Louisville: Westminster John Knox, 2012.

———. *Pneumatology: The Holy Spirit in Ecumenical, International, and Contextual Perspective.* 2nd ed. Grand Rapids: Baker Academic, 2018.

Keener, Craig S. *Gift and Giver: The Holy Spirit for Today.* Grand Rapids: Baker Academic, 2001.

———. *The Gospel of John: A Commentary.* 2 vols. Peabody, MA: Hendrickson, 2003.

Kelly, J. N. D. *Early Christian Doctrines.* 3rd ed. London: Black, 1965.

King, Karen L. *What Is Gnosticism?* Cambridge: Harvard University Press, 2003.

Kruse, Colin G. *The Letters of John.* Pillar New Testament Commentary. Grand Rapids: Eerdmans, 2000.

Lashier, Jackson. *Irenaeus on the Trinity.* Supplements to Vigiliae Christianae 127. Leiden: Brill, 2014.

Layton, Richard A. *Didymus the Blind and His Circle in Late-Antique Alexandria: Virtue and Narrative in Biblical Scholarship.* Urbana, IL: University of Illinois Press, 2004.

Levison, John R. *The Spirit in First-Century Judaism.* Arbeiten zur Geschichte des antiken Judentums und des Urchristentums 29. Leiden: Brill, 1997.

Lewis, Nicola Denzey. *Introduction to "Gnosticism": Ancient Voices, Christian Worlds.* Oxford: Oxford University Press, 2013.

Lieu, Judith M. *I, II, and III John: A Commentary.* New Testament Library. Louisville: Westminster John Knox, 2008.

———. *Image and Reality: The Jews in the World of the Christians in the Second Century.* Edinburgh: T&T Clark, 1996.

Ligonier Ministries. "The State of Theology: What Do People Really Believe in 2018?" 16 October 2018. https://web.archive.org/web/20191201021054/https://www.ligonier.org/blog/state-theology-what-do-people-really-believe-2018/

Lincoln, Andrew T. *The Gospel according to Saint John.* Black's New Testament Commentaries. London: Continuum, 2005.

———. *Truth on Trial: The Lawsuit Motif in the Fourth Gospel.* 2000. Reprint, Eugene, OR: Wipf and Stock, 2019.

Marjanen, Antti. "Montanism: Egalitarian Ecstatic 'New Prophecy.'" In *A Companion to Second-Century Christian 'Heretics,'* edited by Antti Marjanen and Petri Luomanen, 185–212. Supplements to Vigiliae Christianae 76. Leiden: Brill, 2005.

Marx-Wolf, Heidi. *Spiritual Taxonomies and Ritual Authority: Platonists, Priests, and Gnostics in the Third Century C.E.* Divinations. Philadelphia: University of Pennsylvania Press, 2016.

McConnell, James R., Jr. *The* topos *of Divine Testimony in Luke-Acts.* Eugene, OR: Pickwick, 2014.

McCruden, Kevin B. "Monarchy and Economy in Tertullian's *Adversus Praxeam.*" *Scottish Journal of Theology* 55 (2002) 325–37.

McDonnell, Killian. "Does Origen Have a Trinitarian Doctrine of the Holy Spirit?" *Gregorianum* 75 (1994) 5–35.

McGowan, Andrew B. "God in Early Latin Theology: Tertullian and the Trinity." In *God in Early Christian Thought: Essays in Memory of Lloyd G. Patterson*, edited by Andrew B. McGowan, Brian E. Daley, and Timothy J. Gaden, 61–81. Supplements to Vigiliae Christianae 94. Leiden: Brill, 2009.

————. "Tertullian and the 'Heretical' Origins of the 'Orthodox' Trinity." *Journal of Early Christian Studies* 14 (2006) 437–57.

Metzger, Bruce M. *A Textual Commentary on the Greek New Testament*. 2nd ed. Stuttgart: Deutsche Bibelgesellschaft, 1994.

Metzger, Bruce M., and Bart D. Ehrman. *The Text of the New Testament: Its Transmission, Corruption, and Restoration*. 4th ed. Oxford: Oxford University Press, 2005.

Michaels, J. Ramsey. *The Gospel of John*. New International Commentary on the New Testament. Grand Rapids: Eerdmans, 2010.

Minns, Denis. *Irenaeus: An Introduction*. London: T&T Clark, 2010.

Morgan-Wynne, John Eifion. *Holy Spirit and Religious Experience in Christian Literature ca. AD 90–200*. Studies in Christian History and Thought. Milton Keynes, UK: Paternoster, 2006.

Oberdorfer, Bernd. "The Holy Spirit—A Person? Reflection on the Spirit's Trinitarian Identity." In *The Work of the Spirit: Pneumatology and Pentecostalism*, edited by Michael Welker, 27–46. Grand Rapids: Eerdmans, 2006.

Osborn, Eric F. *Irenaeus of Lyons*. Cambridge: Cambridge University Press, 2001.

————. *Justin Martyr*. Beiträge zur historischen Theologie 47. Tübingen: Mohr Siebeck, 1973.

————. *Tertullian: First Theologian of the West*. Cambridge: Cambridge University Press, 1997.

Painter, John. *1, 2, and 3 John*. Sacra Pagina 18. Collegeville, MN: Liturgical, 2002.

Papandrea, James L. *Novatian of Rome and the Culmination of Pre-Nicene Orthodoxy*. Princeton Theological Monograph Series. Eugene, OR: Pickwick, 2011.

Parvis, Paul. "Who Was Irenaeus? An Introduction to the Man and His Work." In *Irenaeus: Life, Scripture, Legacy*, edited by Paul Foster and Sara Parvis, 13–24. Minneapolis: Fortress, 2012.

Pelikan, Jaroslav. *The Emergence of the Catholic Tradition (100–600)*. Vol. 1 of *The Christian Tradition: A History of the Development of Doctrine*. Chicago: University of Chicago Press, 1971.

Presley, Stephen O. "Irenaeus and the Exegetical Roots of Trinitarian Theology." In *Irenaeus: Life, Scripture, Legacy*, edited by Paul Foster and Sara Parvis, 165–71. Minneapolis: Fortress, 2012.

Prestige, G. L. *God in Patristic Thought*. London: SPCK, 1952.

Rabens, Volker. *The Holy Spirit and Ethics in Paul: Transformation and Empowering for Religious-Ethical Life*. 2nd rev. ed. Wissenschaftliche Untersuchungen zum Neuen Testament 2/283. Tübingen: Mohr Siebeck, 2013.

Radde-Gallwitz, Andrew. "The Holy Spirit as Agent, Not Activity: Origen's Argument with Modalism and Its Afterlife in Didymus, Eunomius, and Gregory of Nazianzus." *Vigiliae Christianae* 65 (2011) 227–48.

Ramelli, Ilaria L. E. "Origen, Greek Philosophy, and the Birth of the Trinitarian Meaning of *Hypostasis*." *Harvard Theological Review* 105 (2012) 302–50.

————. "Origen's Anti-Subordinationism and Its Heritage in the Nicene and Cappadocian Line." *Vigiliae Christianae* 65 (2011) 21–49.

Rankin, David. "Tertullian's Vocabulary of the Divine 'Individuals' in *adversus Praxean*." *Sacris erudiri* 40 (2001) 5–46.

Rondeau, Marie-Josèphe. *Les commentateurs patristiques du Psautier Recherches et bilan, 2: Exégèse prosopologique et théologie.* Rome: Pontificium Institutum Studiorum Orientalium, 1985.

Simonetti, Manlio. "Il regresso della teologia dello Spirito santo in Occidente dopo Tertulliano." *Augustinianum* 20 (1980) 655–69.

Skarsaune, Oskar. *In the Shadow of the Temple: Jewish Influences on Early Christianity.* Downers Grove, IL: IVP Academic, 2002.

————. *The Proof from Prophecy: A Study in Justin Martyr's Proof-Text Tradition: Text-Type, Provenance, Theological Profile.* Supplements to Novum Testamentum 56. Leiden: Brill, 1987.

Slusser, Michael. "The Exegetical Roots of Trinitarian Theology." *Theological Studies* 49 (1988) 461–76.

————. "How Much Did Irenaeus Learn from Justin?" *Studia Patristica* 40 (2006) 515–20.

Smith, J. Warren. "The Trinity in the Fourth-Century Fathers." In *The Oxford Handbook on the Trinity*, edited by Gilles Emery and Matthew Levering, 109–22. Oxford: Oxford University Press, 2011.

Stanton, Graham N. "The Spirit in the Writings of Justin Martyr." In *The Holy Spirit and Christian Origins: Essays in Honor of James D. G. Dunn*, edited by Graham N. Stanton, Bruce W. Longenecker, and Stephen Barton, 321–34. Grand Rapids: Eerdmans, 2004.

Steenberg, Irenaeus M. C. *Irenaeus on Creation: The Cosmic Christ and the Saga of Redemption.* Supplements to Vigiliae Christianae 91. Leiden: Brill, 2008.

Stewart-Sykes, Alistair. "The Original Condemnation of Asian Montanism." *Journal of Ecclesiastical History* 50 (1999) 1–22.

Swete, Henry B. *The Holy Spirit in the Ancient Church: A Study of Christian Teaching in the Age of the Fathers.* London: Macmillan, 1912.

Tabbernee, William. "Initiation/Baptism in the Montanist Movement." In *Ablution, Initiation, and Baptism: Late Antiquity, Early Judaism, and Early Christianity*, edited by David Hellholm, et al., 2:917–45. 3 vols. Beihefte zur Zeitschrift für die neutestamentliche Wissenschaft 176. Berlin: De Gruyter, 2010.

Thiselton, Anthony C. *The Holy Spirit—In Biblical Teaching, through the Centuries, and Today.* Grand Rapids: Eerdmans, 2013.

Thomassen, Einar. *The Spiritual Seed: The Church of the "Valentinians."* Nag Hammadi and Manichaean Studies 60. Leiden: Brill, 2006.

Tozer, A. W. *How to Be Filled with the Holy Spirit.* Chicago: Moody, 1952.

Trevett, Christine. *Montanism: Gender, Authority, and the New Prophecy.* Cambridge: Cambridge University Press, 1996.

Trigg, Joseph Wilson. *Origen.* The Early Church Fathers. London: Routledge, 1998.

————. *Origen: The Bible and Philosophy in the Third-Century Church.* Atlanta: John Knox, 1983.

Tzamalikos, P. *Origen: Cosmology and Ontology of Time.* Supplements to Vigiliae Christianae 77. Leiden: Brill, 2006.

Wallace, Daniel B. "Greek Grammar and the Personality of the Holy Spirit." *Bulletin for Biblical Research* 13 (2003) 97–125.

Waszink, J. H. "Tertullian's Principles and Methods of Exegesis." In *Early Christian Literature and the Classical Intellectual Tradition: In Honorem Robert M. Grant*, edited by William R. Schoedel and Robert L. Wilken, 17–31. Théologie historique 53. Paris: Beauchesne, 1979.

Weinandy, Thomas G., and Daniel A. Keating. *Athanasius and His Legacy: Trinitarian-Incarnational Soteriology and Its Reception*. Mapping the Tradition. Minneapolis: Fortress, 2017.

Widdicombe, Peter. *The Fatherhood of God from Origen to Athanasius*. Oxford: Clarendon, 1994.

Wilhite, David E. "The Spirit of Prophecy: Tertullian's Pauline Pneumatology." In *Tertullian and Paul*, edited by Todd D. Still and David E. Wilhite, 45–71. Vol. 1 of *Pauline and Patristic Scholars in Debate*. London: Bloomsbury T&T Clark, 2013.

Wilken, Robert L. *Judaism and the Early Christian Mind: A Study of Cyril of Alexandria's Exegesis and Theology*. New Haven: Yale University Press, 1971.

———. "The Spirit of Holiness: Basil of Caesarea and Early Christian Spirituality." *Worship* 42 (1968) 77–87.

Williams, M. A. *Rethinking "Gnosticism": An Argument for Dismantling a Dubious Category*. Princeton, NJ: Princeton University Press, 1996.

Wright, N. T. *The New Testament and the People of God*. Vol. 1 of Christian Origins and the Question of God. Minneapolis: Fortress, 1992.

Yazykova, Irina, and Hegumen Luka. "The Theological Principles of the Icon and Iconography." In *A History of Icon Painting*, edited by Archimandrite Zacchaeus, 9–28. Translated by Kate Cook. Moscow: "Grand-Holding," 2005.

Young, Frances M. *Biblical Exegesis and the Formation of Christian Culture*. Cambridge: Cambridge University Press, 1997.

Subject Index

Ancient Document Index